THE
AVIATION
ENTHUSIAST

THE REAL AVIATION ENTHUSIAST

BRYAN PHILPOTT

Foreword by Air Chief Marshal
Sir Alasdair Steedman GCB, CBE, DFC

THE
ROYAL AIR FORCE
BENEVOLENT
FUND'S

INTERNATIONAL AIR TATTOO

First published 1987.

*British Library Cataloguing in
Publication Data*

Philpott, Bryan
   The real aviation enthusiast.
   1. Aeronautics—Anecdotes,
   facetiae, satire, etc.
   I. Title II. Lohan, Hugh
   629.13'09'04   TL546.7

   ISBN 0-9511665-0-6

Printed and bound in
Great Britain.

Contents

Foreword

by Air Chief Marshal Sir Alasdair Steedman (Controller Royal Air Force Benevolent Fund and Chairman International Air Tattoo).

We aviation enthusiasts take our passions seriously — you might even justly call some of us addicts — and we tend to frown on anyone poking fun at our specialization. Now this is a pity. A blinkered focusing on the minutiae of even the most fascinating hobby or vocation must ultimately make it pall, and the individual excluding light and humour dull. For building character and tolerance in an increasingly partisan world it is good that we should be made to laugh at ourselves occasionally, and to get a glimpse of ourselves as others see us. That is what Bryan Philpott succeeds in doing in this book.

Few on first reading will fail to raise an eyebrow at a definition of something precious to the reader, and that shows with what accuracy he fires his barbs. 'Using Heinkel 70 Wings for Spitfires' forsooth! But I couldn't avoid a wry smile.

Bryan Philpott is a Real *enthusiast; one of that band of immensely hard working and dedicated volunteers which forms the International Air Tattoo team. They bring pleasure to thousands and much needed money to the Royal Air Force Benevolent Fund.*

The Fund is the means by which the Royal Air Force looks after its own. Eligibility for help from it lasts for life. Rank is irrelevant. If you've served in war or have been a Regular in peace, man or woman, or if you're a dependant of such a person, then you're eligible. Thus the only criterion our independent and voluntary Grants Committee has to con- sider is the existence of distress and what is needed to relieve it. There are no firm rules; each case is considered on its merits, and in confidence. People in distress need help and privacy for their troubles, not publicity.

The range of need and distress is wide. At the top is the

purchase of houses for widows with young children, and for the disabled; at the bottom payment of electricity, gas and fuel bills; there is a mass of problems between. I write this in June 1986. In 1985 we had to give £7,135,469 to 13,044 cases (most of them families). This was 32.4 per cent up on the previous record of 1984. Yet, so far this year, both cases and money given, are up by 20 per cent on the equivalent period of 1985. I don't known how far the requirement will rise. I know the figures for eligibility in the Royal Air Force family and actuarial figures for expectancy of life; but who can forecast how many will need help, and when, and for how much? I do know I can't expect a reduction in pressure on the Fund until the turn of the century.

So, increased fund raising is essential. We must never fail through lack of money to help someone in need. I am deeply grateful to Bryan Philpott and Hugh Lohan for their contributions to this book, the sales of which will be of great help to the work of the Royal Air Force Benevolent Fund. My thanks go also to you, the reader, for in buying the book you not only give yourself entertainment and pleasure, you also help the Fund to help others.

Author's Introduction

Most of us become so engrossed in our jobs, hobbies and pastimes, that too frequently we overlook the fact that there is always a humorous element close at hand. There is a danger of losing sight of this completely and taking ourselves far too seriously, and when this happens a lot of pleasure can go from our lives.

Life is about living: someone once said that it takes fifty muscles to frown but only twenty to smile, so why make work for yourself? Humour is, of course, a very personal thing; what appeals to one person may not appeal to another, but quite often there is a common ground and in the world of aviation this can take many forms.

I have spent many years within the world of aviation during which time it has been my pleasure and privilege to meet the humble and the mighty. This book is an effort to try to lift the lid off some of the people, situations and aircraft I have encountered. There is no malice intended, and if anyone featured takes offence I offer my sincere apologies and would simply ask them to take another look, for in so doing they may well see a part of themselves they didn't appreciate others saw, or they might even identify me in one of the sections where I appear—and I assure you that I do!

Preface

The idea for this book first came to me during the TVS Airshow South at Hurn Airport in 1984. Just outside the Press Centre was parked a Breguet Alizé; its wings were folded and it sat in that rather quaint manner that naval aircraft seem to adopt. Long after the flying had finished, a family group wandered along and stood taking in all the details of this specimen of French aviation. Mum, with the youngest cradled in her arms, was clearly anxious to get home, but dad, complete with his Instamatic, binoculars and picnic box, and a young lad on each hand, wanted his full money's worth. 'What's that dad?'' enquired one of the lads, pointing his ice lolly at the Alizé.

'A Royal Navy Gannet, son,' was the immediate answer.

Meanwhile the other small son had wandered over to our enclosure. 'Is it?' he asked me, clearly doubting dad but not wanting to question his authority.

'Actually, it's an Alizé,' I whispered.

Small boy immediately rushed over to dad shouting, 'No it's not, THAT man. . .' pointing an accusing finger in my general direction, 'says it's a Lizzie'.

Dad looked horror-struck. 'Take no notice of HIM lad. A Lizzie was World War Two plane with wings coming out of the top of the cockpit and a big radial engine. . . THAT's a Gannet.'

Whereupon the whole family turned as one and moved off towards a nearby Jet Provost; my little friend turned towards me and poked his tongue out!

Such groups are what air shows are all about. They are the multitude who make it all worth while, they demand nothing more than a day out in the sun, a lot of interesting things to look at and occupy their time, a spot to sit and enjoy their flasks of tea and sandwiches, and a quiet wander round to see how their taxes are being spent. They make the world of air shows possible and a mecca for that small minority of 'experts', who without any doubt are very knowledgeable, but can also be very painful. Which category are you?

From those small beginnings I started to recall stories

During WW2 the Lysander was renowned for getting into and out of difficult situations. Let's see you get this 'Lizzie' out of this one old chap...

from similar encounters over the years, and at the same time collected anecdotes from colleagues. The IAT team, which over the years has put together what is probably the best military air show in the world, gave me their cooperation and support and were also kind enough to agree to take a substantial quantity of the finished work to sell with all proceeds going to the RAF Benevolent Fund, which carries out so much very important work for those who are, or have been, connected with flying and have fallen upon difficult times.

I should like to thank them all for their support and especially Hugh Lohan whose cartoons have been a source of amusement in the IAT offices and, dare I say it, when surreptitiously passed around at Progress Meetings. Finally, I also thank all of you who have unwittingly found yourselves featured in what I hope you will look upon as nothing more than a little bit of fun.

Bryan Philpott,
Newbury, 1986

This book is dedicated to ALL aviation
enthusiasts wherever they might be...

Aeroplane

Most dictionaries, especially the simplified kind that the reader of this guide is more likely to be familiar with, define the aeroplane simply as 'a heavier-than-air flying machine'. This is all very well but depends a great deal on how the layman interprets the word 'machine'. Since this guide is aimed at those who want to learn all about aeroplanes, the people around them, flying them, the special language surrounding them and the mystique of the world of aviation, this area of uncertainty must be cleared first.

If we look up 'Machine' we find: 'apparatus combining action of several parts to apply mechanical force; controlling body/organization; bicycle, vehicle, motor car, sewing, printing. . .' and so on.

Despite the well intentioned efforts of many well-qualified aeronautical engineers, no-one has yet produced a car that will, at the flick of a switch, become an aeroplane. On the other hand, the 'flying' part is quite true; mind you, not at the flick of a switch but more often the twitch of a steering wheel. Older readers will recall the most spectacular and

'What do you mean. . . you don't think this is the M25?'

successful flight of a Lancia Grand Prix car, when the late Alberto Ascari emerged from the tunnel at Monaco and flew straight into the harbour. Other racing and rally drivers have also found that on running out of track, usually on mountainous circuits, deDion tubes, disc brakes, and independent suspension are poor substitutes for wings, such unexpected flights often ending in very heavy landings; but then in the world of aviation it is said that any landing you walk away from is a good one.

Many a boy racer or motorway maniac, in his Escort 1.6 GL with go-faster stripe, valves bouncing off the pistons, and one hand on his popsy's knee, has also discovered that dreams of reaching for the thigh instead of concentration on the back of the 'artic' in front, have brought a very low-level flight and wings of a different kind. So, the following table is a simple abbreviated guide to what is a heavier-than-air flying machine, but not necessarily an aeroplane in the eyes of the *Real* aviation enthusiast; and you do want to be a *Real* enthusiast don't you?...

'You pulla my tail and I bite...'

'ANY LANDING YOU WALK AWAY FROM IS A GOOD ONE'

'Heavier-than-air flying machines'

Aeroplanes	*Non-aeroplanes*
Most biplanes	All Grand Prix cars
Sopwith Camel	The Spruce Goose
Fokker Triplane	Bristol Brabazon
All DH Moths	Rolling Pins
All long-horns and short-horns (Farman not cows)	Friesians, hunting horns, French horns
Spitfire	P-40 Series
Lancaster	B-24
B-17	Albemarle
Shackleton	Magnus Pike (see helicopter)
Hunter	Any Singer or Brother with or without button hole attachment
Vulcan	DC 10
F-100 Super Sabre	Supermarine Swift
Lightning (EE/BAe)	P-38 Lightning (Lockheed)
Harrier	Javelin (Gloster, Jowett and Olympic)
F-4 Phantom	F-4 Phantom

F-104 Starfighter	F-104G Starfighter (Luftwaffe)
Concorde (British)	Concorde (French)
AWACS	Westhampnett Womens' Institute
F-15 Eagle	Nimrod AEW 3 (fictional at time of compilation)
Super Etendard	TU 104

Some of the entries are duplicated because you will find as you get into the *Real* world of aviation, that different groups of enthusiasts have different views, some even have cults dedicated to one particular type of aeroplane. Entries will appear where appropriate unless members of the group concerned are known to include Henry Cooper, Frank Bruno, Arthur Daley or are bigger than the author.

Aircraft

An up-market word which covers all types of flying machines, unless you hear it uttered in 'East Enders' when careful listening will reveal that what has been said is ''aircraft', meaning the skill of hairdressing in cutting, colouring or styling; not often seen in aviation circles.

Airships

Once considered to be the air transport of the future. But that was back in the days when the aeroplane was a collection of spruce, canvas and wire. Used extensively in the First World War to drops bombs, but where these fell was guesswork, since navigation was at a very early development, as is proved by the German airship captain who though he was over London but later discovered that it was the lights of Paris beneath him. It is rumoured that in the early days of aviation the French spent all their budget on building the biggest mooring mast for airships in the world, then had no money left for the actual machines. But they had the last laugh as the Eiffel Tower, as they called it, has probably attracted more money to the country than travelling suspended under two million cubic feet of highly inflammable hydrogen would have done.

Following the disastrous conflagration which ended the life of the *Hindenburg,* plus the crash of the British *R101* (both at one time blamed on sabotage by George Peppard and/or Humphrey Bogart) the appeal of travelling by a fire looking for somewhere to start not surprisingly waned. Those on the fringe of aviation knowledge will often give their limited expertise away by talking of airships as zeppelins; this was the manufacturer of a type of airship (Count von Zeppelin) and is a general generic term often used by non-*Real* enthusiasts. All enthusiasts will try to pretend airships never existed; proved by Led Zeppelin which is a contradiction as all airships are 'Lighter-than-air flying machines'.

Aerobatics

Most aeroplanes are designed to perform efficiently with the pilot sitting upright and the wheels pointing down when—in the case of an aircraft with a retractable undercarriage—they are lowered and the aircraft is straight and level to the horizon. But in the very early days of flight the Russian aviator (they were not called pilots then) Petr Nestrov, was quietly cruising above the Volga playing his balalaika when a wasp stung him in a very embarrassing place. In trying to reach the affected area, he managed to get all the controls out of order and carried out the very first loop the loop. From then on there was no holding the more adventurous and gradually a whole repertoire, with the help of the Royal Ballet, was developed, and today it is not unusual to see aeroplanes in all sorts of positions relative to the line of

flight. This is nothing to be alarmed about unless:
(a) You are a passenger;
(b) The aircraft is a Boeing 747, or indeed any airliner;
(c) You have no parachute or ejection seat;
(d) When you finally look up the pilot has gone.

Most enthusiasts will boast about the aerobatics they have flown, but cover a mile quicker than Sebastian Coe when offered a trip in a Pitts Special.

'That's the trouble when you get Australian pilots on TDY.' (NB, TDY is an American military term for Temporary Detachment.)

Airlines

Until you become really involved in the world of aviation you will probably think that an airline is something you use when your car tyres need pumping up. When you are converted, not only will you know this is true, but also that it covers that field of mass transport which claims to be the safest way to get from a to b, in most countries where life is regarded as precious, and in fact is. Every country of note or standing has its own airline, and in addition to the major ones there are usually many smaller or feeder lines. There is a whole group of enthusiasts who spend all their time logging movements of airliners throughout the world. The activities of those who are still roaming freely on the outside of detention centres or mental institutes, will be dealt with later. Meantime a short assessment of some of the more familiar airlines, most of which advertize regularly on television, does not seem out of place.

TWA
Will fly you anywhere in America for £25 providing you agree to film with your own Super 8 cine, and travel back by Greyhound as they own the majority of that company's shares. You must also be prepared to wear funny hats, fall into the Grand Canyon, and show your home movie to anyone who is in the slightest bit interested.

PAA
Make sure that you can fly from any country in the world to any destination that does not have electrically operated doors where you will be trapped with two suitcases, as you struggle to find there is more to life than a Harvey Walbanger or a chat-up from a fugitive from 'Dynasty'.

British Airways
Has managed to turn a giant trading loss into an enormous profit by training stewards and stewardesses—collectively known as Cabin Staff—to fly without aeroplanes. This means they now formate with the company's aircraft and

feed the passengers through the windows. They are also adept at catching briefcases, and playing with footballs on motorways (Arsenal FC please note). But with up to ten staff no longer needed on the *inside* of a '747 it is easy to see how ten more fare-paying passengers on every trip and every route, has enabled the Chairman to buy a new Sinclair C 5 every month, and give the staff a regular bonus. The latter might prove costly since it is now rumoured that all '747s have to have structural modifications to the bulge above the pilot's cockpit, unless BA can persuade flight crews to discontinue their age-old habit of sitting on their wallets.

British Caledonian
Like BA have increased their profits but by even bigger margins simply by persuading their passengers that they can fly *without* aeroplanes. They sit them on conveyor belts—to help the illusion of movement—and get a tartan clad dolly bird to show them how to stretch their arms outwards at 90° to the body, sway from side to side, and carry their luggage on their laps.

Air Canada
Will fly your cat to any destination in the world and put it out just as the milk arrives. How they have avoided prosecution by the RSPCA is their secret. Whether or not they will be able to maintain this record when passengers start leaving the aircraft after landing, is open to some conjecture.

> If you worry about how the crew know where to fly the aeroplane, just remember that in daylight at the height you are flying, they can see for miles and none of them wear spectacles. At night, if you glance out of the left-hand side windows you will see a *red* light, and out of the right-hand ones a *green* light; all the crew has to do is stay between the two.

If you are nervous about flying, always try to take your own bomb along. The odds of flying on an airliner with a bomb on board are 1,750,000 to 1. The odds of flying on board an airliner with *two* bombs on board go out to 117,000,000,000 to 1.

Aeroflot
Has a total monopoly, therefore adds real meaning to the phrase 'Go to Jail' if you stop on the wrong (Red) square. Always makes a profit because under a multi-lateral government agreement it must carry all spies, dissidents and members of CND out of the country. So if things begin to look tough Comrade Boss just declares all Western embassy staffs are spies and they are deported. Negotiated a deal with the Americans to also do this from the USA especially in the case of those who ask for political asylum then see the light and change their mind and wish to return to Russia, usually via Siberia. It is understood that the American agreement was only reached providing Aeroflot removed the Sukhoi 25 from their Korean route, which was non-profit making anyway.

Air France
In an endeavour to recover the government's loss in building the biggest airship mooring mast in Europe, then failing to make it a tourist attraction when the *Hindenburg* brought a crash to airship shares and an increase in those of fire extinguisher manufacturers, is clipping the wings off all its aircraft, welding the fuselages together and making a two-way Channel tunnel. Surplus jet engines will be used to create continuous force ten gales to keep all ferries and hovercraft in port.

Lufthansa
Without any doubt Europe's most efficient airline, probably due to experience gained in mass transportation techniques

during the days of the Luftwaffe which was an important part of its formative years. A break with old-established tradition is that, although most of their fleet still have three engines, they have done away with corrugated skinning.

Qantas
Must be named Bruce or Sheila to be employed by this airline, and have knack of scrounging corks to hang from strings on flight crews' hats, since they only serve Fosters straight from the can. Believed to make all their money from government contracts to fly Australian cricketers (*all of them* since the 1985 Ashes series against England) to and from South Africa; that is, when seats are not occupied by Koala bears.

Air Singapore
Guarantees total attention from a cabin staff of thousands. All adverts show only the silhouette of one passenger in the window of a '747 as it fades into the setting sun, with an infinite number of Chinese birds waiting to pounce.

All Chinese airlines
Fierce competition among this group to see who will be the first civil operator of the C.5 Galaxy. It is a well-known fact that as passengers enter this aircraft in China, they would multiply by a factor of ten, and a new generation would be born every time the nose crossed the equator whilst the tail was in Peking. Believed to be part of a proposed co-operation deal with El Al leading to long term contract work leading to ever-growing profits (see El Al).

Never, never stand up and start gathering your hand baggage before the 'Fasten your seatbelt' sign goes out. This only causes delays since passengers milling about in the fuselage obscure the pilot's rear view when he wants to reverse on to the unloading ramp.

> Always try to find the location of the 'black' box (it is, in fact, bright orange) since if they expect to recover this in the event of a crash, there must be a better than average chance of survival if you are sitting above it.

El Al

Another airline showing a marked increase in profit margins achieved by charging passengers for their tickets *after* the flight. This enables the rate of inflation during the duration of the flight to be taken into account. With this running at about 130 per cent in Israel, where all policy decisions are taken, it is easy to see how profitable a four-hour flight can be.

Aer Lingus

It was rumoured that in the interest of economy they had asked Sinclair to design an electric-powered '747, but the cost of the wander lead proved prohibitive so the project was abandoned. They are reputed to have now invested in a fleet of Vickers Valencias in which they have so much faith that they have named them after famous ships from history, the first three being the *Mary Rose*, the *Marie Celeste* and the *Titanic*.

Have also made a bid for the spare Concordes held by Air France, since the management has worked out that four hour's flight time to New York instead of the current eight (both times allow for Irish navigation) will reduce their wages bill for cabin staff and flight crews by 50 per cent.

South African Airlines

Most airlines have two classes, First and Tourist; but with SAA it is not easy to make such a black and white division. The only major airline that carries coloured instead of 'B***K' boxes for accident investigation.

Air Traffic Control

'C'mon lads. . . who pulled the plug and left me high and dry?'

Since the dawn of aviation everyone wanted to be a pilot. This is, of course, not possible, so to avoid disappointing a lot of people Air Traffic Control was created. These men and women are like traffic wardens, but far more important can (whisper it) walk on clouds. They stop aeroplanes from flying all over the sky, and make them follow routes down narrow corridors, thus increasing the chances of them bumping into each other, but conversely increasing the importance of their job. These corridors, or airways as they prefer to call them, are all colour-coded, as it is known that very few pilots can actually read.

When an aeroplane takes-off the Air Traffic Controller will tell the pilot to 'Climb to flight level 2, and enter Green One at seven'. This is pure jargon that only he understands, but it means that pilots cannot be colour blind and must spend their time looking for a *green* corridor; it is not possible to paint the sky green so eventually he gives in and the Air Traffic Controller will give the secret away by telling him that he must head south-south-east at 2,000 feet for seven minutes. Everyone is now happy since this has taken enough time for the next aeroplane to be far enough behind the first to stop it bumping into it. So the Air Traffic

Controller has earned his keep. They all live in a building with a glass roof, useful for growing tomatoes, and some of them have radar sets as well as lots of telephones. They will be dealt with under RADAR.

Air Correspondents

All *Real* enthusiasts are well advised to totally ignore anything written or said by those working for the popular media under the above titles. Their knowledge of aviation is usually inversely proportional to their consumption of free food and drink. This is not too surprising because the daily news media is only interested in air crashes, hi-jacks, the odd air record that may be broken, or the collapse of airlines, aircraft and/or helicopter manufacturing companies. Most air correspondents have much more important journalistic jobs such as writing obituary columns, or fetching tea for the social diary column writer. They will appear at air shows, demanding the earth, not understanding anything they see and complaining about having had to wait to get in,

the gin is too cold or too hot, there is not enough food, and wondering if Mrs Thatcher, the Minister of Defence, the Duke of Edinburgh or Samantha Fox are going to attend.

Signs to watch for are: they always want a telephone on arrival, will refer to anyone who flew in World War 2 as an *Ace* even if he was only a u/t pilot on Tiger Moths, and believe that the whole air war was fought by Spitfires, Lancasters, Messerschmitts and 'einkels. Best summing up of their breed was once given by a military aviation liaison officer (Fleet Air Arm) who was heard to utter after a particularly difficult conversation with a BBC Air Correspondent, 'They're all bone from the knee up... and that's flattering bone'.

Real Air Correspondents
Grading out of ten:

Bo Derek	10
Frank Robson	0
Richard Colthard	0
Christopher Wain	− 8
Geoffrey (not Jeffrey) Archer	1
Michael Donne	1
Arthur Reed	2
Michael O'Toole	− 8
James Wilkinson	0
Ellis Plaice	0
Roger Bray	0
Harvey Elliot	0
Vladimer Grovoski (*The Guardian*)	0

Daily national newspapers with *Real* Air Correspondents: *Pravda, Istvetzia.*

Air Shows

This is such a wide subject that it will be covered under

separate related headings covering all the elements that make-up a genuine *Real* Air Show. Meanwhile, here are some of the main criteria:

Real Air Shows are usually held on days that are, wet, windy, showery, and sometimes, occasionally, very very hot. Good organizers will arrange for all the above to be present throughout every day, thus giving hot-dog, ice cream, summer wear and arctic survival wear vendors equal opportunities to fleece (sorry) sell to enthusiasts.

A lot of thought has to be given to the venue which must be: surrounded by minor roads that can easily be blocked at peak times by tractors, harrows (not Handley Page version, unless at Shuttleworth) and/or combine harvesters, as well as fringe groups demonstrating about anything vaguely connected with war or aviation.

Air Show organizers can easily be recognized by the number of 'OFFICIAL' badges they wear or have on their cars; a useful guide is that their importance is usually inversely proportional to the quantity and size of badges carried.

Great care has to be taken in selecting a date that will coincide with some anniversary connected with milestones of aviation history; for example, the discovery by Howard Carter that Lord Carnarvon was von Richthofen's batman, Pontius was in fact a navigator, Magellan was an Air Electronics Operator, and the Spitfire was designed by Willi Messerschmitt and sold to Vickers to pay off a gambling debt... there are many others listed in the Greek orthodox translation of the *Koran*, which is available free from the Royal Aeronautical Society to air show organizers.

Balloons (Hot-Air)

The lift element for a balloon being supplied by a three man all-party House of Commons Select Committee formed to discuss the future of British Aviation.

The earliest known form of air travel, especially for animals. They consist of a big bag (no comment) under which is slung a basket (no comment) above which is a gas burner directed by the crew into the big bag thus filling it with hot air to provide lift.

They have no form of guidance, drift along with the prevailing wind, stay well under cover when the going gets tough, have no idea where they are going, frighten old people and animals, and have no recognizable useful purpose; the closest aviation ever gets to politics.

Crews are usually very confident people more associated with red-coats (horse not Butlin variety), wear Puffa or Husky jackets, green wellies and eat cucumber sandwiches. More at home listening to 'The Archers' (not Jeffrey) or at Badminton or Smith's Lawn, where they stay when conditions are bad for ballooning—usually 360 days every year except Leap Year when it is 361.

Endless sources of supply of lift element can be obtained from: Air Correspondents listed on page 26 (except Bo Derek), Nigel Dempster, William Hickey, Jean Rook, Mrs Thatcher, Arthur Scargill, Esther Rantzen, Neil Kinnock, David Owen, David Steel, Murray Walker, Bill MacClaren, George Gale, Shirley Williams, Bobby Robson, HRH The Duke of York, Prince Philip, Ayatollah Khomenie, Don Howe, John Motsom, Jimmy Hill, Mary Whitehouse, Joan Ruddock, Bruce Kent, any Australian (especially when their cricket team is winning), Terry Wogan, Rev Ian Paisley, Madonna, any French Prime Minister, Ian McGregor, Minister of Defence, Chairman of Westland, NASA, TV AM or Michael Grade.

Books

Of the thousands of aviation books published every year the following will give the *Real* enthusiast the true background to the rich panorama of aviation history:

Biggles at Kittyhawk, by Charles Gibbs-Smith
Biggles at War 1914-1918, by Chaz Bowyer
Biggles at Halton, by Chaz Bowyer
Biggles at War 1939-1945, by Alfred Price
Biggles and the Spitfire, by Alfred Price
Biggles and the Lancaster, Vols 1 to 10, by Brian Goulding
   & Mike Garbett
Biggles at Action Stations, by M.J.F. Bowyer
Biggles over the Desert, by T.E. Lawrence
The Encyclopedia of Biggles' Aircraft, by Bill Gunston
Biggles' Guide to Air Power, by Bill Gunston
Is Bill Gunston Biggles?, by Chris Chant
Is Biggles Bill Gunston?, by Mrs Gunston
The Aircraft Illustrated Extra Guide to Biggles, by Peter
   March, Danny March, Andrew March, Granny March,
   Grandad March, Aunty Bertha March, Route March,
   Allin Adays March, with translation from the French by
   Frog March.
Biggles was Black, by Bernie Grant
Biggles was White, by Enoch Powell
Biggles was to BS 381C, by Ian Huntley
Biggles Saves Westlands, by Michael Heseltine
Biggles. A worthy successor to Margaret Thatcher?, by
   Jeffrey Archer
Biggles in the Falklands, by Brian (I counted them out)
   Hanrahan
Biggles in Space, by Patrick Moore
Biggles Flies the Foxbat, by A.E.W. Nimrod (A young
   child's Fairy Story)
Biggles was Gay, by Ken Livingstone
Giggle with Biggles, by Joan Collins
I Married Biggles, by Elizabeth Taylor
Budget with Biggles, by Derek Hatton
Biggles Fights Apartheid, by Nelson and Winnie Mandela
Is Biggles God?, by The Archbishop of York
God is my Co-pilot, by Biggles
Is Biggles in the Brotherhood?, by F. Mason.

Biplanes

All the early pioneers failed with monoplanes, Icarus being a classic example, so when Orville and Wilbur Wright succeeded in making the first heavier-than-air aeroplane fly, and it was a biplane, everyone decided they must be right, their surname also helped this conviction. The truth of the matter is that the Wrights were bicycle makers so naturally opted for two wings as well as two wheels, but more importantly they were working along the same lines independently and when they decided to join forces didn't want to waste their completed work so used both sets of wings. For nearly forty years aircraft designers thought only of biplanes mainly because:

In open cockpit aircraft the top wing helped keep the pilot dry in wet weather, and cool in hot weather;

The Wing Assemblers' Guilds (WAGS) were able to keep members happy with double employment. Producers of

'I vas damn lucky Herr Colonel. Der vas ten auf dem, and wun vas Mister Biggles.'

Most REAL enthusiasts love the fresh air. At the wing walking school the first easy steps are taken on an open top bus. . . very few graduate to the ultimate. Those that do get a very good view of every air show.

bracing wire never had it so good;

As motor cars carried a spare wheel, it was only logical that aeroplanes should carry a spare set of wings;

Useful employment was provided for wing strut makers;

The top wing gave wing walkers something to hold on to, and girls could stand on them at air displays to produce *oohs* and *ahs* from the crowd, and the pilot if she happened to choose a short skirt!

The gradual introduction of only one set of wings was helped by the Second World War, since as production increased the demand for one set of wings per aeroplane was equal to the pre-war requirement of two, so unemployment—especially among WAGS—was not noticed until after the war. The attempt by Lockheed to introduce aeroplanes with no wings (ie the F-104) was a failure, so the monoplane rules supreme although many enthusiasts (see under Shuttleworth) still dream of the beauty of the biplane and conjecture about a double-deck Tornado or even '747...

Canard

This is included because it is one of those rare and weird designs that *Real* enthusiasts fall in love with, and literally must get their teeth into. This type of aircraft is built back-to-front and is believed to be the sole example of co-operation between the the French and Irish. Rumour is that the Irish designer Shamus O'Cart-Befor l'Orse was contracted to produce a small experimental aircraft for the French but read the drawings backwards. This resulted in the tailplane being at the front of the aircraft and the wings at the rear. Only a few manufacturers took any interest in this revolutionary design, although there has recently been a revival since, as the name is derived from a delightful recipe for *duck*, thought has been given to the design of an airliner specifically aimed at taking and returning Australian cricketers on tour anywhere, and English ones to and from the West Indies.

To date there are only three members of the 'Make a Canard Club' (MCC), but the authorities have asked the author not to name them in case of reprisals by other inmates.

Cameras

The camera and its associated equipment is vital to all *Real* enthusiasts. It must be a 35 mm SLR made by Nikon, Minolta, Pentax or Canon, and at least four bodies with twenty interchangeable lenses are *essential*. This means that any black/white or colour film can be instantly available in a body, it then just becomes a question of fitting the right lens, setting the correct speed and aperture, in a few seconds as action unfolds before you. This of course takes years of practice, but do not despair as all the photographs with fuzzy edges can be sold to *Janes* and other magazines as 'A picture taken in secret of the latest Russian combat aircraft'. All Russian aircraft are photographed in dull weather and they are all built with ragged edges to the wings, fuselage

Whenever you want a clear unobstructed picture, there is always someone who MUST put his head, body and even legs, down the intake or up the jet pipe. This one should be warned that Jaguars sometimes eat people!

The new Jumbo-size REAL enthusiast photographers' step ladder undergoing functional tests by Danny, Andrew and Peter March. Most DIY stores have home assembly kits on offer for £55 plus 28 covers from Aircraft Illustrated Extra *(Photo Mrs March).*

and tailplanes.

A step ladder is also necessary so that if you are short you can see over the heads of those in front of you at air displays, and if you are tall, you can take good pictures of the tops of aeroplanes. Dwarfs are usually employed by photographic agencies to get under aeroplanes, so there is little market in selling pictures of this type. An aluminium case to carry films, filters, lens, tripods, bipods and lens hoods is also essential although its real purpose is for the display of stickers. All this means that the best pictures of aeroplanes, especially at displays, are taken by normal people with Olympus Trip type cameras. But if you want to be seen as a *Real* enthusiast, you must have the genuine trappings.

Major problems faced by enthusiastic photographers at

displays and other aviation venues are:
Getting display pilots to appreciate just how hard it is to
photograph their aircraft if they go too fast;
Getting organizers to hold their displays in good weather;
Getting a position where the sun is in the right place all
day when the organizers do manage a good day;
Getting the paying public to keep their heads out of
tailpipes of jet aircraft, air intakes of all aircraft, posing
against wings, tails, rockets, drop tanks and cockpit steps,
whilst 'dad' records the happy event with this Polaroid;
Getting a Press Pass;
Having enough strength to carry all the equipment;
At airports, getting airliners to park close to the public
viewing area, and taxi slowly.
     The rewards are great and can include:
Selling a picture to *Aircraft Illustrated* for as much as
£5.00;
A rejection slip from *Aviation News*;
Getting one of the enthusiast specialist publications to
print a perfectly good picture and make it look as though
it has fuzzy edges and appear to have been developed in
Oxtail Soup;
Winning an Olympus Trip in a photographic competition.
     Whatever else happens you must keep trying, because
there is more to aviation photography than just *flashing*
your stickers.

Civil Aviation

This is a branch of aviation that the majority of people are
familiar with since they come face to face with it when they
go on holiday or on business trips. It attracts a totally
different type of *Real* enthusiast than military aviation and
these range from the type who spend every waking moment
in the public viewing area of his nearest airport, to those
who are well heeled enough to spend every waking moment

'Number...?'
'Rank...?'
'Name...?'

at the *Club* (flying of course), flying or talking about Cessnas, Pipers and various extinct tribes of American Indians (most popular American light civil aircraft are named after these). So you have now taken your first step to being able to understand this sort of conversation:

'Hello old boy. Just saw Tompkins put a Cherokee down slap bang in front of that Apache, bet the CFI has something to say. But of course I understand no one told him the Red Arrows were using the field for a low-level pass at the time. Damn bad show, wouldn't have got away with it in '40 you know.'

One of the unsolved mysteries of the world of the civil aviation enthusiast is why so many of them collect fiction in the form of airline timetables, aircraft registration letters or put adverts like this in magazines like *Aviation News*: 'Can anyone help Salford spotter with reggie of unknown airliner that flew over Manchester at 45,300 ft at 13:13 hrs on Sunday 14 February 1982?'

It could be that on a package deal to Majorca in 1979 he lost his luggage and is trying to trace it, a bit fell off the passing airliner that he is anxious to return, or he wants to know what type of binoculars anyone who can answer his question was using... who knows... and dare we whisper it... who cares?

Real civil aviation enthusiasts can be spotted because:
They will have a pair of binoculars around their neck;
At least 23 pencils and five notebooks in a tatty sports bag;
Thick wool pullovers, woollen hats and woolly socks outside their jeans (in *all* climates);
Their necks will be at a constant angle of 45° to the horizon.
Their ambitions will include:
To be arrested at Moscow Airport;
To be arrested anywhere behind the Iron Curtain;
To be a member of the Mile High Club;
To receive an erotic note from a Aeroflot stewardess on a package trip to Siberia;
To become eccentric enough to join the ranks of *Real* military aviation enthusiasts.

Camouflage

A colourful yet dull aspect of aviation that you must have some knowledge of, especially if you are a model maker. It is well known among *Real* enthusiasts that it is the main reason why the Allies won the Second World War, the Germans were second, and the Italians unplaced. Although hundreds of books have been written about the subject, it still appears on a regular basis in all types of aviation magazine.

Basically, all aircraft during war and peacetime are painted in some colour or other that will, in theory, tone them into their surroundings. This is a tall order, for when they are on the ground they have to look like a tree, a desert or a bush, when they are in the air they have to 'disappear' into the blue/grey/white/ blue yonder. The most successful attempt at camouflage occurred on 5 December 1945 when five Grumman TBM Avengers took off from Fort Lauderdale in Florida and were so effectively painted that they have never been seen since; this gave birth to the famous Bermuda Triangle legend.

During World War 2 the Allies and Germans constantly issued instructions as as to the patterns and colours aircraft would be painted; the experts tell us that this was *so* important that the war would temporarily end whilst each side looked for the right colour. Until recently it was believed that the turning point in the Battle of Britain came when the Luftwaffe switched their point of attack from airfields to London, but the following document recently found in the PRO proves this to be wrong:

'Order 40/FC/RAF/ADMIN/No 525 issue B date 3 September 1940.

'All fighter aircraft will effective from this day, be painted brown and green on their top surfaces each colour to be to BS 381c issue 5, each colour to be five shades lighter than the present brown and green to BS 381c issue 4, the undersides to remain sky-blue.

'All units to acknowledge.'

On receipt of this instruction all first-line fighter squadrons had to ground their aircraft whilst the 'Chief' could locate supplies of the right colours. The result was that the Air Ministry (as it was then) had to telephone Luftwaffe HQ in France and get Göring to call a halt to proceedings until every Spitfire and Hurricane was the right colour. This he readily agreed to do as the 'Camouflage Agreement of 1938', signed in Geneva, was binding to all nations. It will be readily appreciated therefore that paint was a vital ingredient in the war and if more effort had been made by both sides to destroy paint works, especially those involved in research into colours, the war could have ended much earlier.

Today, it is still vitally important and the greys, greens and blues favoured by modern military aircraft are all to a British or American Standard and *must not* be deviated from. At least, that is what all the self-appointed experts say, and who are we to disagree?

If there is a sign of recession in the paint trade, civil airlines under a Government directive will change their colour schemes; as it takes five tonnes of paint to cover a Boeing 747, it is easy to see how this helps the economy.

The following is just a very simple guide to the layman of the complexity of the system; there are 285 pages to learn if you want to be a *Real* enthusiast:

Proper colour ref	*Layman's colour*
BS 381 C:638 Sea Grey	Grey
BS 381 C:627 Lt. A/C Grey	Grey
BS 381 C:637 Med. Sea Grey	Grey
BS 381 C:697 Lt. Blue Grey	Grey
BS 381 C:18B21 Semi Matt Grey	Grey
FS 595a:36440 Gull Grey	Grey
FS 595a:36231 Dark Gull Grey	Grey
FS 595a:36473 COIN Grey	Grey
FS 595a:36622 Grey	Grey
and so on...	

Concorde

The only supersonic airliner in service in the world, apart from the Russian one which only carries cattle and mail. It has enabled British Airways to show a profit and Air France to complain more and more about the British. It has also enabled more people to fly at twice the speed of sound than there are military pilots who can claim the same. It is faster than most military aircraft, so if a war should break out the safest place is on board a Concorde, book now as it is doubtful if any politicians appreciate this. It is very popular with clergymen since at the height it flies, it is only a local call for them to 'phone the Boss.

Rumoured to be of Anglo/French design but the French actually only contributed the complementary copies of *The Day of the Jackal* and onions used in the pre-cooked in-flight meals. Concorde pilots can be identified from their companions on other aircraft because they do not have LEFT and RGHT tattooed on the backs of their fingers.

Concorde can be chartered for practically any event and a prized possession of all *Real* enthusiasts is a certificate to show they have a) seen it, b) touched it, c) been photographed in it, or d) flown in it. The latter to them is much more valuable than three membership certificates of the Mile High Club.

A recent innovation is to use the aircraft for crop spraying; it will be expensive but can cover ten counties in less than four minutes.

Normally use for crop-spraying in Texas, this B52 adds that unmistakable barbecue flavour to a camper's breakfast.

'I don't care how you got in, it's still £5.00 to park including all occupants.'

'They tell me the police are hot on illegal parking in this area.'

Dress

At some time or another all *Real* enthusiasts will be seen wearing:
Green zip-fronted anorak with orange lining;
Baseball cap; Jeans;
Doc Marten boots; Light blue trainers;
Anoraks with fur-lined hoods and lots of 'patches'—badges, to the unconverted—sewn on them;
Zip-boots;
Blazers with military buttons and badges;
Squadron, Command or RAF (with aircrew motif) ties;
Cardboard cut-out gift caps in hot weather conditions only;
Military-style woollen pullovers with reinforced patches at elbows and shoulders, bought at Millets. Rarely with epaulettes, and more often RAF Blue or navy, very rarely Khaki;
Bow ties but definitely *not* clip-on type;

Check shirts;
Paisley cravats;
International Air Tattoo (IAT) ties or metal badges;
RAF or Luftwaffe squadron scarves;
White silk scarves if more inclined to USAF;
Silk stockings with black seams, if more inclined to USAF;
Black tights; Black leather blouson and matching trousers if inclined towards World War 2 Luftwaffe, plus monocle if *really* dedicated;

A typical REAL enthusiast in full wet weather gear. The life jacket is mandatory in most British summers. . .

46

Deer Stalker, plus fours and Norfolk jacket (Shuttleworth Open Days only);
Tee shirts with aeronautical legends across front;
Leather jackets, brown fur-lined with colourful paintings on back, if leaning towards World War 2 USAAF, usually worn with sunglasses, even if the rain is belting down;
Green flying suits with only one patch sewn on left-sleeve at shoulder;   String vest, only with above;
Open toed sandals and socks, only with green flying suits;
Camouflaged combat jackets and matching trousers, with *no* patches sewn on;
Marks and Spencer shiny material blue blouson with patches sewn on in every spare space.

All the above apply equally to male and female *Real* enthusiasts, depending on degree of conversion either has reached from influence of partner.

The *Real* enthusiast will *never* be seen wearing:
Grey pin-striped suit with RAF tie;
Brigade of Guards or RCT tie;
REME tie, unless it is replacing belt on combat trousers;
Tee shirt with a Building Society name or logo across front or rear;
Building Society cardboard cut-out hat in hot weather;
Camouflaged combat coat *with* patches sewn to it;
Suede shoes with corduroy trousers;
String tied just below knee of any type of trousers;
Green Husky jacket;   Beige Puffa jacket;
Flat cap;
Bowler hat, unless at Trooping the Colour;
Straw boater, unless at Henley for meeting of Tiger Moth Seaplane Club;
Mk VIII goggles with new style crash helmet;
Barbour coat;   CND badge;
White roll-neck sweater;   Fleet Air Arm tie;
A straitjacket.

Displays

The increasing popularity of aviation is reflected in the number of air displays held in the summer months throughout the world. These go under a variety of names, a few of which to guide you are listed:

Name of event	Real enthusiastic rating
SBAC Display, often called simply *Farnborough,* held every two years.	A must, especially for civil aviation enthusiasts and those who actually want to buy aeroplanes or military hardware. Stain your face a light brown and wear a turban for top attention, or a jibban for absolutely undivided attention. Extra effect can be obtained by getting girlfriend to wear a veil, and cutting off left hand.
IAT. This is the International Air Tattoo held every two years at RAF Fairford.	A *must* for all but the absolutely avid civil nut. People travel from every corner of the world not so much for the eight-hour flying display, but to travel in open top buses to take photographs of the tops of aeroplanes, without any fear of interruption. Suitable attire is anything listed under Dress.
RAF Open Days.	OK if one is near you but not really worth travelling miles to see mainly old aeroplanes hurrying from base to base, to create the illusion that the RAF still has a lot of aeroplanes and does not only fly on Wednesdays.
Royal Navy Air Days.	A must for helicopter fans, but don't expect to see the famous

The flying control committee ensures that all pilots fly within safety limits and do not break the rules. Any that disobey are immediately grounded.

'Are we staying the WHOLE weekend skip?'

'Are you 100 per cent sure that bit came out of there?'

'Do you HAVE to keep singing, ''Put some oil in my lamp keep it burning''....?'

Navy trick of landing a Sea Harrier on Spanish freighter. This has only been done once, and that was to publicise Trafalgar Day.

Army Air Days.

If you go to a Navy Day forget this unless you want to see the same helicopters painted different colours. Unlikely to see anything humorous like a helicopter replacing the Queen for the ceremony of Trooping the Colour.

USAF Open Days.

An essential part of the tyro *Real* enthusiasts' education programme. A festival of F-111s, F-15s, F-4s, F-14s and F-all, but the hamburgers and root beer, if you like liquid germolene, are out of this world.

Shuttleworth Open Days. Held regularly throughout the summer months, usually clash with a Test Match or Wimbledon, but never Ascot or Henley.

Dust off the Morris Eight series E or the 4½-litre Bentley, and go back to a forgotten age. Only likely to see funny aeroplanes with two sets of wings, a fan device on the front, and lots of people in Edwardian Dress carrying

'I shall be glad when cigarette manufacturers stop sponsoring us.'

'I'm not worried about HER... it's what the RSPCA might do.'

	wicker baskets and shooting sticks.
The Great Warbirds Display.	Fine for those who want to see pop stars trying to be display pilots, old World War 2 preserved aeroplanes, and the Red Arrows, who of course manage to get in on most displays.
Aerojumble.	Not strictly speaking a flying display, but held at the home of the FAA Museum, and gives the *Real* enthusiast a chance to acquire good memorabilia at inflated prices which will not be noticed because of the local environment.
RAFA Displays. Frequently throughout year but check local press.	Great care in selection needed. Can be a full-blown display, or just a fly-past by the Red Arrows, or the Branch

THE MAN WHO MISSED SHUTTLEWORTH, FARNBOROUGH AND (YES, SERIOUSLY, I KID YOU NOT) I.A.T !!

Potential customers at a recent auction at Shuttleworth when a push-rod from a WW1 aero-engine came under the hammer. It is estimated that 5,000 photographs of the component were taken and these will be worth at least 25p each in years to come.

Chairman in his twin Apache. Take a chance if you are a gambling addict.

Air Races. Frequent throughout year.

Once again not really flying displays but a chance to see lots of civil aeroplanes, some of which will be refurbished military aircraft, flying very low, at all sorts of speeds, and trying to arrive at the same place at the same time, despite starting at different intervals. Mainly for participants wishing to escape the restrictions of Air Traffic Control. *Not* essential viewing.

Cranfield Meet.

Fine for civil spotters, and those wanting to buy light aeroplanes, otherwise forget it.

'Harry.. are you sure that's not the Mk III Jack Russell we saw at the Light Aircraft Rally?'

There are, of course, many displays throughout the world that go under a variety of titles ranging from Air Pageant to Air Spectacular. There are superb shows in America, held at places with unbelievable names such as Oshkosh, Harlingen, Indian Springs and Reno; Paris and Ramstein also feature as do some Middle East Countries, who usually disguise their displays as full-scale wars. As you become converted, you will develop your own fetish and from the reading material you buy, will decide where to go and what to support. But remember that to be socially acceptable you must be seen in the right dress at IAT, Farnborough and Shuttleworth at least once. This is like going to Ascot, Lords or Smith's lawn to see whatever it is they have at those places.

Designations

The world of aviation is littered with abbreviations, mnemonics, definitions, simplifications, slang and jargon. It is not necessary to know all these but a few, apart from slang and jargon which will be dealt with separately, are shown as a guide:

BUFF   Big Ugly Fat Fella—B-52 bomber

SLUF	Short Little Ugly Fella—A-7 Navy/Air Force fighter
MRCA	Must Refurbish the Canberra Again, or Mother Riley's Cardboard Aeroplane—Tornado
FRED	Flaming Ridiculous Economic Disaster—C5 Galaxy
TWA	Try Walking Across
QANTAS	Quite a Nice Touch-down. Any Survivors?
BOAC	Better On A Camel
BAL	Bring A Life-jacket
SAHSA	Stay At Home Stay alive
TACA	Take A Chance Always
TAN	Tough And Nasty
BWIA	Britain's Worst Investment Abroad
Triple Threat	Bombs you, Strafes you, Falls on you—Harrier or F-105

Aluminium Overcast—Vulcan or B-36

'Sure I can read the bottom line......I...P...T...B...M...'

55

Enthusiasts

Aviation enthusiasts form themselves into groups, societies, clubs, and organizations, most of which reflect in their names the particular field in which they are interested as well as the subject they cater for. Spotters have been touched on under civil aviation, but there are many others and the following is meant to be only a general guide, since in some cases greater details are given within different headings. This might be complicated to the reader, but it will give a good grounding as most enthusiast groups turn out to be that way anyway.

Airframe number collectors
All military aircraft have airframe numbers which can be referred to as tail numbers, buzz numbers, serials, codes and a hundred-and-one other definitions, some of which are wrong, but it doesn't really matter as, to quote a well known collector, 'A rose by any other name...' Enthusiasts, like the civil registration letter collectors, collect these, copy them into notebooks, cross-reference them, memorize them, categorize them and quote them at every opportunity. Do not be surprised to learn that whole books listing them have been published, and if you can imagine page after page after page of lists of numbers, then you are on the track of a bestseller. This aspect of the hobby is probably as close as it is possible to get to the age-old hobby of train spotting and car number collecting.

At air displays they will be seen noting *every* aircraft on the ground, in the air and hidden in hangars. Some will use a tape recorder and walk down the lines mumbling into it such phrases as '*XR783,* Lightning F-6, No 5 Squadron Binbrook, seen Fairford 14 July 1985, two-tone grey, tail code *AE* in white, intake rim silver polished...' and so on. This will all be logged in a book or these days on a micro-computer, and appear in a letter to *Aviation News* in ten years' time when someone misquotes a Phantom as having code *AE* and serialled *XR783*. Never, never, question the authenticity of these people unless you have at least two hours to spare for each question.

Preservation Groups
See under **P**, meanwhile a short aperitif. The Magpies of aviation enthusiasts. Will find any excuse for trying to collect, and restore to pristine condition, anything connected with aviation past, present and sometimes future.

Aviation Archaeology Groups
A relatively new type of enthusiast group owing its existence to the advent of the metal detector. Members will go to endless lengths, and in fact depths, to extract unrecognisable bits of twisted and scorched aluminium and other trivia from deep holes where aircraft are believed to have lost the ceaseless struggle against gravity.

A byproduct is often the establishment of some form of museum, quite often a shed in a garden, in which are displayed the pieces recovered. Many such groups do a roaring trade with others in supplying parts they do not need or have surplus of. As a result of these activities there is hardly an aviation museum in the country that does not own a part of the Dornier Do 17Z of Hauptmann Roth of KG76 that was shot down near Biggin Hill in the Battle of Britain and is known as the 'Leaves Green Dornier'. If all these parts were re-assembled there would be enough to recreate the whole of KG76.

Similarly, many groups and individuals also have parts of the framework of the first 'Zeppelin' to be shot down at Cuffley; the fact that this was a Schütte-Lanz which had a wooden frame, appears not yet to have been noticed by the metal detector brigade. Recent achievements have been the recovery of a Halifax from the bottom of a fjord in Norway and a Wellington from the bottom of Loch Ness. Both aircraft, so we are told, still had the crew's sandwiches on board in an edible condition. There is some danger involved in this type of work, as what is often not recorded is that after a recent excavation in Norfolk of a B-24 it was found

'Now you guys. . . remember these enthusiasts will try anything to get in. . . . some might even offer to pay.'

that the electrics still worked; these were connected to a battery and blew the whole lot sky high as the bomb load was also still aboard. A search is going on for five enthusiasts, a JCB and two innocent bystanders. But the explosion, which also killed 5,000 turkeys, had its compensations when Bernard Matthews put £10,000 up front to fund a similar search.

If grovelling about in mud in green wellies is for you, then this is a part of aviation you cannot afford to miss out on.

Historical Groups
Usually less inclined to be physically active and prefer to meet in pubs or hotels to talk about the last two World Wars. Quite often include members of the Air Gunners' Association and the Aircrew Association. Often have long and somewhat heated debates as to why in World War 2, if you were in Bomber Command you got the DFC/DFM after thirty trips in a Lancaster or Halifax, but if in Fighter

Command, you had to have thirty Spitfires or Hurricane shot away from under you to receive similar recognition. Love to be united with German aircrew and appear with arms around each other in photographs in the local press showing that bygones are bygones. It is not often reported that once they are well 'tanked up' it is not unusual for BMWs in the car park to have indentations that closely fit Ford bumpers and Aircrew Association car badges.

(NB. The Air Gunners' Association seems to multiply but as this aircrew category has not been recruited since 1953 it is just a myth, which proves that a) anyone could be an AG or b) not so many of them were killed off as popular World War 2 fiction would have us believe.)

There are many other historical groups and they include long established organizations such as:

Air Britain. Within this organization there are many separate groups each totally dedicated to a specific aspect of aviation such as: the colour of Herman Göring's underwear; the interior colour and design of the Chipmunk in which HRH Prince Philip, Duke of Edinburgh, learned to fly; the colour of the Exocet missile decoy helicopter flown by HRH The Duke of York at the time of the Falklands; to whom Westlands are going to sell the Blackhawk helicopter.

They also publish *Air Britain Digest* which has no Humour in Uniform section, but lots of lists of numbers that have been specially selected for regular readers.

Air Wales. Has only two groups, one specializing in ground-attack aircraft used against cottages owned by people who are not Welsh Nationalists, the other in trying to prove that the Wright brothers were Welshmen. It is essential to be able to speak the Welsh language to become a member.

Air Ireland. A small group which studies the strategic use of the submarine in air warfare, and invented the inflatable dartboard.

BARG. This group studies movements of all horse-drawn longboats on Britain's canal systems, as well as all movements of aircraft in and out of the British Isles, both civil and military. All airlines as well as MoD(Air) are members as it enables them to keep track of the aeroplanes they own. Produces lists of all aircraft movements and publishes them in a monthly magazine which looks like a telephone directory without names. They also attend air shows and make a lot of money by selling lists of all aircraft on display, those not on display, those that wanted to come but couldn't, and those that will be along next time round.

Groups encourage all types of enthusiasts to become members and therefore differ from societies which are rather more up-market (see any dictionary for confirmation); these will be dealt with under **S**. Actually, the main difference is that members of societies have to wear a tie to meetings. There are many overseas clubs, groups and societies for *Real* enthusiasts, but perhaps the most well-known is:

The Confederate Air Force. Based where else but Texas... Members are usually enthusiasts who own at least two oil wells, a million acre smallholding, and ten old World War 2 aeroplanes; but being a democratic organization anyone can join by paying $500, donating thirty empty Coke cans, or ten used LPs of Dolly Parton, Billy Jo Spears and/or Crystal Gayle.

On being accepted every member becomes a Colonel thus ensuring total equality... (and these guys hate Communism!).

Any member who crashes three of his own aircraft and one of another member, receives an immediate award of the Cross of the Golden Spittoon, and if in the process fires-up an oil well, the decoration is enhanced by the ribbon of the Yellow Rose of Texas.

Founder members include Ben Lyon, and Ronald Reagan from whom full membership details can be obtained by sending a self-addressed stamped envelope or IRC to the White House. Do not forget to add your ZIP code.

Ejection Seats

As you become more knowledgeable about aviation you will find there are many aspects that you might want to delve into. Aircraft equipment can be a fascinating study so various parts are included under relevant headings. One of the most interesting is the Ejection Seat. This is a device that is fired from military aircraft only, and enables the crew to make a safe parachute descent from any height, at any speed, when something goes wrong. It is very useful when the weather is bad since most military aircraft glide like housebricks when they run out of fuel or the engine(s) stop for any other reason. The seat therefore gives the safest, and sometimes only, means of survival. Aircrew who have used it can be recognized because they wear ties with little red triangles on them, are usually at least two inches shorter than they were, have flat tops to their heads, and speak in high-pitched squeaky voices.

It is thought that Martin-Baker, the manufacturers of the most successful seat, have recently been awarded a contract to install them in the Cabinet Room at 10 Downing Street, to enable the Prime Minister to give dissenting Ministers an immediate lift to higher offices.

'Touch me there again and I'll scream.'

FOD

An abbreviation standing for Foreign Object Damage. Very rare at British airports, apart from Leeds/Bradford, but common, as one would expect, on European and Middle East airfields. Notices are displayed to be aware of it, so it is just as well to be careful to throw any litter such as beer cans, old car jacks, bits of preserved or recovered aircraft, into the proper receptacles, especially at air shows where a good wind can turn the whole lot over and make a thoroughly good job of spreading it about. Care has to be taken at airfields where displays are being held as there can be a good attendance of uncontrollable foreigners. On such occasions volunteers are usually lined up to march across the field collecting everything in sight.

This is another example of the rewards awaiting the *Real* enthusiast, for on such occasions the show organizers, who themselves always find they have been called to a vital meeting at the time the FOD walk is about to begin, usually manage to toss the 'volunteers' a can of beer and a wrapped quarter pounder, thus creating the need for another FOD walk and another urgent meeting... and so on *ad infinitum...*

Flying Doctors

These can be Australian doctors who are pilots flying from one part of Australia to another to prescribe a tube of Fosters or tend to sunburned backsides; especially during visits by overseas Royalty. Or they can be a plane-load of GPs flying to Miami to study the effect of liquid transplants on the human liver which cannot be done in Bradford, Manchester or Slough. The major difference is that the former will be flying a Ford Trimotor of 1935 vintage and operating from Wollamboola base with a 'Sheila' up front, the latter will be on board Concorde with a 'Sheila' in 69 places administering G & T on the NHS.

Films

To the *Real* enthusiast films are next best thing to air shows, and the arrival of the video has made those long winter evenings much more bearable. To become a *Real* enthusiast you must be able to spot errors made during filming and quote these to fellow enthusiasts or anybody who cares to listen. The overall authenticity of the film is of minor importance, as is or was the availability of correct props (not revolving types, that was the producers' problem). The following are just a few of the films regularly seen on the silver screen, or the TV, with a few hints of what to try and spot:

The Dam Busters	Wrong radar aerials on Lancasters, Lincolns making up numbers in background.
Battle of Britain	Two-seat Spitfire, Susanah York's 1969 vintage suspenders. Henderson up-and-over garage door... if you are still interested after looking for previous error.
The Blue Max	Tiger Moth.
Hell's Angels	Avro 504K, Boeing Stearman.
Journey Together	George Cole without Terry McCann.
633 Squadron	Post-war Anson, the wrong mark Mosquito,
Mosquito Squadron	...you are a glutton for punishment.
Aces High	Inserts from *The Blue Max*.
Reach for the Sky	The change in Kenneth More's limp.
The One That Got Away	Train in post-war BR livery, but biggest error is that it is running to time.
BBC Documentary on IAT '85	BBC commentator getting two consecutive facts right.
Fighter Squadron	Luftwaffe pilot speaking German without American accent.

A colour scheme that will cause endless arguments as to the right BS or FS colour code for FLESH.

'Just let ME go and slip into something a little more comfortable.'

The lamp standard slalom is a new manoeuvre the Red Arrows are trying for the 1987 season.

'It's either seaweed, in which case we are underwater, or its trees and someone's moved the sea.'

DRESS FOR REAL ENTHUSIASTS

We couldn't hit the runway at Port Stanley from 30,000 feet, so what chance have we of getting ALL this into that little sock?'

The Bridges at Toko Ri.   Grumman Panther in two shades
                             too light midnight blue.

There are many others which have all been listed in a short
booklet entitled:
What to look for to spoil your enjoyment of aviation films
which is available from the Lands End Aviation Buffs Film
Appreciation Club, for £35 (hardback) or £55 (softback).
Cheques, cash, money orders (NO credit cards) to: The
Keeper, The Lighthouse, Lands End, or Charles and Ronny
Kray c/o HM Prison, Pentonville.

Food

When *Real* enthusiasts have time to eat they select from the
following: Cheese and onion flavoured crisps; Do'nuts
(without the ugh); Hamburgers; Beefburgers; Cheese rolls,
never with pickle; Egg and salad cream sandwiches; Heinz
beans (cold) (unless going flying); Hot soup, *never*
Minestrone; Cucumber sandwiches and strawberries and
cream (Shuttleworth only); Chips with all of above.

'The skipper DID warn
Minelli about taking
too much garlic.'

It can be dangerous to take pets to airshows. . . they sometimes recognize relatives on the fast food take-away stalls.

On special occasions the RAF police will often look the other way. . .

Never knowingly have Lasagne, any Chinese take-away, curry, or other food that might make you seek the 'Loo' during the flying display or feature film.

Never have any tomato ketchup, or any form of relish, vinegar or savoury sauce that might run over camera lens, notebooks, or into tape recorders.

Always drink lager or coke, *never* tea or coffee from a plastic cup.

Finally, *never, never* eat a USAF packed lunch, these have far more value in their natural and original form (see under Memorabilia).

Friends of International Air Tattoo

These are a bunch of dedicated *Real* enthusiasts most of whom are members of *every* club, group or society mentioned in this book, but deserve their own separate entry, mainly because they wouldn't pay the author and

cartoonist a large sum of money to be kept out...

Members of F.I.A.T., as it is known, are not fugitive robots from a well-known Italian car maker, they come in all shapes, sizes, colours, creeds, and callings but all have the following in common:

...they all worship at the Shrine of IAT every two years, all love travelling on open top buses, all have at least ten SLR 35 mm cameras and eight lenses, all have a former U-boat Commander's binoculars, all can recite the BARG participants at IAT shows lists for the last ten years, all love to be herded into an enclosure where they can stand for four days, talking, sleeping, living, and dreaming aviation, and if lucky sniffing Avtur or Avtag, are the nearest seen in England to a plague of locust when a) the gates to the airfield are open at some unearthly hour in the morning, b) the Lancaster or Vulcan lands at the far end of the airfield from their enclosure, or c) someone announces that the organizers have not yet managed to get the barriers around the SR 71.

They are the only known human species totally feared by RAF Police dogs, either singularly or collectively... But they are the epitome of the *Real* enthusiast and without them aviation probably wouldn't exist, at least not as we know it today.

French Aircraft

Until 1939 all French aircraft looked like bird cages with wings and engines, from 1939 to 1950 none existed, from 1950 to 1982 looked like beer barrels with wings and engines. From 1982 to date, not discussed by *Real* enthusiasts because of activity in South Atlantic.

'The Red Arrows may have
done over 2,000 performances
in the air, but when it comes to
the SAC... the
THUNDERBIRDS have 'em
beat... Aint that so Hank?'

I always come before James
Bond to check the goods.

Girls

Members of the female sex tend to feature more as art-work on World War 2 American bombers, as pin-ups in crew rooms, or draped around certain aeroplanes for publicity purposes. However, if a female *Real* enthusiast is wearing the right clothes (see under Dress) it is very difficult to detect her, so firm conclusions must not be drawn. The majority of those who are discovered will:

Know more about aeroplanes than their male counterparts...

Be more attractive than their male counterparts...

Wear tighter jeans than their male counterparts...

Have a better eye for camouflage—although they will call it a colour scheme—than their male counterparts...

Have much more success in persuading pilots to show them close-up parts of their equipment than their male counterparts...

and have a better chance of becoming members of the Mile High Club than their male counterparts.

It must be pointed out that the above does not apply to members of the Womens' Armed Forces, who because of the original military sex equality act of 1815 (see *Mother Ross at Waterloo,* published by Heinnemann), are indistinguishable from their male counterparts.

Gliders and Gliding

Apart from strapping wings made from feathers to the arms and leaping off towers, gliders are the oldest known form of heavier-than-air aircraft. Glider pilots wear woolly hats with coloured bobbles, thick jumpers, lightweight trousers and Adidas trainers. They spend all their time talking about lift, thermals, cloud formations, rate of sink, ridge soaring, and retrieving.

The glider or sailplane is towed into the air by another aeroplane with an engine; by means of a long steel cable attached to the nose and hauled to 900 feet by a tractor; by huge rubber bands throwing it off the side of a hill; or by its own little engine stolen off the lawnmower (which gives as good an excuse, as any, for not cutting the grass). Once airborne gravity does the rest; usually fairly quickly in the case of beginners.

Those who aspire to this type of aviation can pay to go on a week or two-week holiday at a gliding school where they will be told that running about collecting tow cables from all over the airfield, driving the retrieving tractor, walking at wing tips, the weather being too bad for them to fly and making tea are all essential parts of the gliding world and must be mastered before they can take to the air. By the end of the second week, providing all members of the resident club have had at least twenty flights, the newcomer just *might* be given a two minute ('fancy that, the tow's broken') experience flight.

This should not be confused with military gliding which has a small, but important part in aviation history. Briefly, all the participants in World War 2 found that it was cheaper to make plywood aeroplanes without engines and tow them behind transport aircraft, than it was to make lots of the latter and parachutes to fit airborne troops who were trained to leap from them at the sign of a green light. So infantry soldiers were persuaded by a smooth-talking PR man that parachuting was dangerous and it was much safer to be towed in a plywood packing case with wings behind an old aeroplane and land in comfort at their objective, rather than be scattered all over a 'drop zone' by parachute and have to fight individually to join up again with colleagues to form a powerful fighting unit.

Those soldiers who were very poor shots and had little co-ordination were usually selected to be glider pilots. The glider thus saved a lot of money in metal aircraft, aero-engines and parachutes, as well as providing raw material for camp fires. Those conveyed in gliders now know that what they were told was not exactly true, as at the first sign of trouble the tug pilot usually cast them adrift, the impact with the ground usually cast them just as far apart from each other as a parachute descent, and the plywood burned equally as well in the air as on the ground.

This method of taking troops into action was abandoned after World War 2, although the failure of the Irish parachute, which opens on impact, has prompted the Irish Army to re-open investigations into glider transport. Glider pilots can usually be identified by their short legs, scarred faces and chewed finger nails.

Ground Equipment

A very minor part of aviation but the *Real* enthusiast always tries to gather some knowledge so that he can make the

'Yeah — wouldn't put anything past those low-down Ruskies — but we're ready for 'em.'

casual throwaway comment when wandering around airfields—for example: 'I see they're using a 5 mW GEC genny now instead of the old trolley acc'. This means nothing to those who have no knowledge, but creates a good atmosphere of well being at being accompanied by a right know-all. It doesn't really matter if the identity is not 100 per cent correct but some care should be taken to get the general idea since even the dimmest usually know the difference between a portaloo and a runway controller's van. (For the unitiated, the latter is usually painted in black and white checkers, if not, then it is *hard* to tell the difference in the example quoted.)

—Gremlins——————————

Well known to all aircrew in World War 2, they were little people who mysteriously interfered with aircraft at vital times, such as obscuring windscreens, re-setting pitch controls from fine to coarse and *vice versa*, putting undercarriage levers back into 'UP' or 'DOWN' after the opposite had been selected, filling clouds with mountains, etc, etc. They still exist today but are usually more subtle in their interference with aviation-related matters, a few examples being:

any Minister of Defence,   David Steel,
Lord King,   Ronnie Reagan,
Chief of the Air Staff,   Preservation Groups,
Flight International,   the BBC,
TV AM,   Noel Edmonds,
Terry Wogan,
Jimmy Young (Shuttleworth aircraft only),
Colonel Kadaffi (Israeli aircraft only),
the Army Air Corps
and Ken Livingstone's GLC* (before abolition).

*Gremlins Love Conservatives.

Horses

It could be Ascot or Badminton...

Since the dawn of aviation horses and aeroplanes have just not mixed. The Army took an instant dislike to the aeroplane for frightening cavalry horses, and the rift has never been repaired. This is why you will never see the Queen taking the salute at Trooping the Colour from any type of aeroplane, or the Red Arrows appearing at any major equestrian event like Horse of the Year Show, the Derby or the Grand National, although they have been asked to be curtain-raisers at practically every other type of sport.

Helicopters

In the same way that magicians over the years have deceived audiences with demonstrations of levitation or the Indian Rope Trick, the helicopter continues to prove that it is not necessary to have wings to fly. This really is an illusion and it is amazing how many people fall for it. *Real* enthusiasts look upon them as just a small part of the world of aviation and as they carry codes, numbers, and different paint schemes, they might just as well include them within their sphere of interest, but you will never get a *Real* enthusiast to fly in one, they take their guide from HM The Queen who is rarely allowed to travel by this type of aircraft. To put the whole thing into perspective just consider that the machine, which can weigh anything up to ten tonnes, is lifted into the air by rotating blades which are held to a drive shaft by eight 10 BA bolts... would anyone in their right senses go near one?

Most children and some adults—mainly passengers of British Caledonian—are very good at pretending to be aeroplanes by running about with their arms stretched parallel to the ground, and making engine noises with their lips. Those with large elbows make particularly good DC3s, Heralds and Fokker F27 Friendships. The helicopter provides much greater scope for such talents, among those very gifted at helicopter impersonations being:

Adolf Hitler,   Neil Kinnock,
Magnus Pyke (his twin rotor Chinook is very good),
Roy Hattersley (does a rather nice line in any type of helicopter flying low over water),

I thought they only did that to dogs.

Michael Heseltine (noted for his falling Blackhawk),
Cyril Smith (the whole British helicopter industry),
any English cricketer trying to stop a West Indian hitting
sixes,
Bruce Grobbelaar,
Bill Gunston (after reading the entry under books),
Peter March and family (ditto),
Elfan Ap Rees,   Paul Beaver,
General Galtieri,   most Harrier pilots
and all male Pop Stars.

Hovercraft

A British invention so in many ways it must be better than
what the Wright Bros are usually credited with. This craft is
a cross between an aeroplane, ship and helicopter, thus it
combines the best of three worlds. It only flies at very low
level, so is popular with the speed merchants, travels equally
well over land or sea, but has not wheels or floats, so is
puncture-free and not subject to being tossed about like a
cork, and relies on a cushion of air to support it, so does not
need wings or deception like the helicopter.

Not popular at air shows as it makes a lot of noise and
creates a lot of dust, the hovercraft is generally regarded in
aviation circles as interesting but not of any great
significance... nor of any great military use since, like a
woman, once its protective skirt has been penetrated, it
becomes uncontrollable...

Harrier

Popular at air shows because it makes a lot of noise and
creates a lot of dust. Another British invention so it must be
good. Can do everything a helicopter can and has wings, so
it *must* be a real aeroplane.

'I'm sure I spotted a Spanish freighter.'

Things the Harrier can do:
fly forwards, backwards, upwards, downwards, sideways,
quickly, slowly, the Waltz, the Gay Gordons, the Hokey
Cokey;
land on Spanish freighters at sea;
ski uphill faster than the Austrians can downhill;
shoot down Mirages, Skyhawks, Canberras and Pucaras,
especially if they have Argentinian pilots;
prove how strong its main undercarriage is if its engine fails
in the hover mode; and
attract crowds to air shows (except Shuttleworth).

Things the Harrier cannot do:
rescue Michael Heseltine from the back benches;
the Tango, Rumba or Flamenco
glide, hover inverted, except in Australia
carry as many cans of Coke as an F-111
walk on water despite what many *Real* enthusiasts might
believe.

Impressed Aircraft

Whenever war looks imminent Governments who have skimped on buying military aircraft look around to see how many suitable civil aircraft they can 'borrow' for the duration. In more leisurely days this was not difficult as there were many aircraft privately owned that had close performances to military machines or could be adapted for use as trainers, or craftily exported to a potential enemy before the start of hostilities under the guise of being the latest military weapon. Today this would prove difficult, so as a guide to Governments a survey recently taken among *Real* enthusiasts is published below for the first time:

Civilian-registered aircraft that could be impressed	*Suggested use*
Total Shuttleworth Collection.	Missile decoys.
Total FAA and RAF Museums collections.	Re-equip current FAA and RAF front-line squadrons.
All privately owned F-104s.	Export to potential enemy as docile trainers.
Concorde.	High altitude transport or bomber.
All helicopters.	Exocet missile decoys.
Nimrod AEW 3 (just the one owned by Hawker Siddeley).	Export to potential enemy as latest in Early Warning Radar aircraft.
All Spitfires.	To be used by the SAS in an attempt to prove that the current vogue of 'knocking' the aircraft's achievements in World War 2 is a campaign by the 'Support the Hurricane Society'.
All World War 1 replicas.	To convince enemy pilots they have flown into a time warp situation, forcing them to abandon briefed mission.

In an attempt to upstage the AA, the RAC now have a new method of recovering broken down vehicles.

Italian Aircraft

All Italian aircraft are biplanes rigged with spaghetti, except bombers which use macaroni. Very highly manoeuvrable, and popular with pilots... presumably because in the event of a forced landing they can be eaten. Very rarely seen since monoplane designs became popular. Modern Italian aircraft differ from most other countries' designs as they are fitted with 'HEAD DOWN' displays rather than 'HEAD UP'.

Israeli Aircraft

Made to a strict budget so are usually copied from other designs. Identified by very large noses and enormous intakes... the latter mainly because air is free. Always have a built-in box of homing pigeons trained to tow remains back to Jerusalem if pilot is fatally injured. Never fitted with self-destruct devices, and always have triple back-up systems to save any part however small it might be. Only known military aircraft to use rockets, ammunition, and air-to-ground missiles with refund fee on empty cases. Long-range fuel tanks can be jettisoned, but are fitted with parachutes for recovery and have reward for return. Useful recognition feature is that tailpipes are often well cut-back.

Icarus

The very first *Real* aviation enthusiast, who with his father Daedulus, set off to fly from Crete to the Greek mainland with wings made from genuine bird feathers. These were held to their arms by wax, and in the exhilaration of flight Icarus flew too close to the sun, the wax melted and he became the first victim of flight. Like many pioneers and *Real* enthusiasts, his enthusiasm dangerously exceeded his technical know-how. It has since been established that he couldn't have flown *THAT* high without oxygen so is more likely to have flapped his wings too fast, went through Mach 1, and encountered the Heat Barrier. But no one is likely to re-write Greek legend to account for his demise in a true and accurate manner.

COME ON DAD, I SPENT AGES MAKING IT.

Jets

SOME FOOL STARTED THE ENGINE!

There are *Real* enthusiasts for every type of aeroplane: some like jets while others like propeller-driven aeroplanes and some like both; the latter are in the minority. It is very rare for a propeller 'man' to also be keen on 'jets'.

Jets are planes that do not have that cooling fan thing going round at the front or on pods on the wings. They suck air, and anything that gets in front of them, into their insides where they churn it all up, set fire to it, and spit it out at the back. There is a fatal fascination for both the front and rear end of jet powered aircraft among *all* members of the public when they attend air shows. They will first find an aircraft that is easily reached and then, after looking all round to make sure that at least a hundred *Real* enthusiasts are trying to take photographs, will stuff their heads up the tailpipes or intakes of the engines. Fortunately most of them do know when the engines are running, but there is going to be a memorable day when one of them overlooks this necessary precaution and ends up very warm and spread across the airfield. This will be extremely messy but it will solve all future problems of this type and enable the *Real* enthusiast to take his pictures without heads or legs doing a vanishing act in holes where they shouldn't be.

Japanese Aircraft

Ever keen on economy, the Japanese learned very quickly that it was wise to make their aeroplanes with less instruments, less crew comfort, less armour, less metal, in fact less of everything than western equivalents. It quickly followed that further weight could be saved by persuading the pilot that a parachute was also totally unnecessary—especially since in most cases he was going on a one-way trip anyway. Today, they have abandoned this approach, much to the relief of crews and passengers of all Japan Airlines, especially when they operate a Japanese-built and -designed aircraft, which in itself is a rarity. Their apparent lack of interest in the world of aircraft manufacture, however, should be ignored, because they quickly learned that there was a much bigger and better market in producing high quality aviation magazines with top rate colour pictures—all taken with Japanese-made 35 SLR cameras—sold to western world enthusiasts.

Some notable examples of *Real* enthusiast magazines with good colour pictures that sometimes feature the delicate Japanese shape are: *Playboy, Penthouse, Mayfair, Fiesta, Men Only, The Watchtower, The Warcry,* and *The Cheadle & Chumley WI Gazette* (colour supplement).

Journalists (aviation)
(see also Air Correspondents)

Aviation journalists should *not* be confused with Air Correspondents. Journalists in the main know what they are writing about, but in most cases they in fact know too much or at least think they do. This is known as the KA (Know-All) factor. Most of them have grossly inflated opinions of just about everything connected with aviation including themselves. This is known as the EF (Ego Factor). The KA factor divided by the EF gives the BF (Bore Factor), the ideal being to get a BF of 1 which gives a top rating. The reader can amuse himself by calculating the BF for any aviation journalist simply by applying his own figures to the KA and EF components. As a guide, all the following—by no means a definitive listing—should have a BF of one or better if you have worked out the combinations correctly:

Bill Gunston, Christopher Chant, Alan W. Hall, Chris Pocock, Lindsay Peacock, Jerry Scutts, Chris Ellis, Charles Caine, Mike Gething, Richard Riding, Malcolm English, John W. Taylor, Michael Taylor, any other Taylor, Peter March (etc), Arthur Reed, Richard Ward (the other one!), Michael Donne, Ian Huntley, Gordon Swanborough, Tom Hamil and any editor of *Air Mail*.

Every journalist has a BF factor but modesty prevents the author from including his name and many others, as he feels that either the KA or EF components will make it too difficult for the reader to arrive at any satisfactory conclusion.

Junk

In the late 1960s various governments throughout the world became aware of a serious situation that was facing many scrap metal dealers, so they introduced a policy of cancelling all types of projects in which there was some tangible evidence of progress, thus releasing vast quantities of raw material to scrap metal dealers. In some respects this can be traced back to wartime days when many different types of aircraft were produced and became useable *junk* to scrap dealers either at home or abroad. This policy is known to have continued until 1982 when the Argentine Government (or those pretending to be such a body), sent a force of scrap dealers to the Falkland Islands to see if there was anything belonging to the British that they might profitably use to bolster the Argentinian economy. The following are examples, that over the years have played important roles in this type of government strategy:

R100,	*R101,*	RE8,	Junkers Ju 87,
Heinkel He 112,		Manchester,	Albacore,
Fulmar,	Battle,	Airacobra,	Buffalo,
P-38,	The Brabazon,	Meteor NF 11,	Attacker,
Tudor,	Swift,	Brigand,	Buckingham,
P-1121,	TSR2,	Avro Arrow,	

the Australian Aircraft Industry,
the Iranian Air Force,   the Irish Air Force,
the Egyptian Air Force (mainly in 1956),   the Sinclair C 5,
the 1986 MCC Tour of the West Indies,
and the Libyan Air Force after their victory in March 1986 over the US Sixth Fleet.

Jargon

There are many variations of the language of aviation, and the *Real* enthusiast will need to learn the Phonetic Alphabet as *all* Jargon is based on the total understanding of this. This

'I must ask you to blow into this bag sir. . .'

'I said, "what a big STICK"...'

alphabet can be found in many publications, especially those related to scouting so it will not be repeated here. If you intend to use a radio tuned into aircraft frequencies, you must become familiar with many different types of jargon, spoken with many different accents, but all with the same aim; to cause absolute chaos. To learn how to understand jargon it is wise to use a simulator; this can be simply a vacuum cleaner howling in the background whilst your wife, girlfriend or other companion, cups their hands and shouts through them into a plastic carrier bag, whilst stamping their feet and pulling the cat's tail. This will create an authentic background.

The following is typical jargon with alternative translations:

'Gatwick Approach... Good morning, this is Alfa Romeo Tango, inbound, advise QDM, QNH, and RVR.'

This means:

'I am calling the Approach Controller at Gatwick, my call-sign is A.R.T., I am coming in, and I want to have a course to steer, the barometric pressure and the runway visual range.'

It will sound like this:

'Gatwishaprosssssh, goomornssh, isshis AlaaaRomeoTngoooooo, grrrrrrrssshpppp, adshhhhh, QDMQNHRVRsspgr, ssh sssh, click.'

What it actually means is:

'Hello sailor; I am unattached, driving an Italian sports car; can you direct me to *Come Dancing* and Peter West, what's the competition like, haven't we met somewhere before?'

The reference to QDM and QNH are legacies from a code that was used in the heyday of wireless telegraphy, when it took a long time to transmit messages in full so a code was devised to shorten them. This eventually led to the aircraft having to carry such a big book of translations that it proved more effective to teach wireless operators to read and speak, and use a microphone instead of a Morse key. It was another case of jargon nearly ruling the world. It is *not* necessary for the *Real* enthusiast to learn the 'Q' code.

Joy Stick

This is an old-fashioned term for what is now known as the control column which is what controls the up and down movement of the aircraft; the joy stick still exists and controls up and down movement but is now more commonly known as... (censored!—Ed.)

Killing Time

As with most things, there are times in aviation when not a lot seems to be happening. At Air Shows there are intervals between demonstrations, and when travelling by air passengers have to check-in a long time before flight departures. Both these examples are to give the *Real* enthusiast time to look around, inspect the aeroplanes not flying, and check out the one he/she is going to fly on. Once this art has been mastered there will be long periods when there is not a lot to do apart from killing time. This is done by wandering around with eyes glazed, a blank expression, hood over camera lens, pencil and notebook stowed, and mouth closed.

It is vitally important not to stay like this for too long otherwise you might be mistaken for a member of: CND, Freeze, Greenpeace, an aviation group, a society, the Press, an aviation photographer, a politician, a football supporter, a member of the CID, an Australian cricketer or worse still, an Air Show Organizer.

Kite

A long time ago people on the outside of aviation all believed that those on the inside called all aeroplanes *Kites*; DO NOT use this expression, it will date you. A kite is a paper device attached to a string and flown on windy days, mostly at Hampstead Heath in London, or anywhere in China, by men who want to get out of the household chores. It can sometimes be used by Air Stewards (either sex) to indicate deafness. They will be seen to lean very close to a passenger's lips, then step back with a startled expression on their face, and be heard to say, 'Go fly your kite'.

Knot

After World War 2 it was decided that all aeroplanes would

travel at a rate of knots rather than mph, so *Knot* is a term used to define this as well as certain pieces of hardware that were rendered scrap by the actions of a former (1982) Minister of Defence, hence it can be said that the *Belgrano*, the Argentinian Army, Navy and Air Force, were 'Knotted'. It is also used by some less sophisticated airline cabin staff than those mentioned above, when the expression, again to indicate a certain hearing weakness, is: 'Get Knotted!'

'One way or another, there's going to be a mighty bang...'

Luftwaffe

This is a subject much loved by all aviation enthusiasts, probably because it has every ingredient necessary to make those long, dark, cold, winter evenings times to be cherished. There are so many books written about the activities of the Deutsches Luftwaffe (to give the subject its true heading) that the enthusiast need never step outside until the start of the Air Show season. Coupled to this is the fact that during this time it is almost certain that the BBC or ITV will repeat for the nth time *Where Eagles Dare*, which has some good air-to-air photography of a Ju 52, *633 Squadron* and its Bf 108, not to mention the possibility of *The Battle of Britain* and all those disguised Spanish aeroplanes and radio-controlled Ju 87s. But the main reason is that the Germans just loved to give not only their aeroplanes but also their serving units long strings of seemingly meaningless numbers, all of which are the meat in the sandwich for the *Real* enthusiast. They are also delighted by the many changes of paint schemes and camouflage used, so it does not require a great deal of imagination to understand why this period is the one that has generated the most groups, societies, historians, authors and self-

'It leaks around the cockpit at low level, but it's still under warranty.'

After the war some German shadow factories were overlooked. 'Ein moment Herr Hermann, I shall finish by 1952!'

appointed experts.

Those likely to know the least about it are: the German Embassy, The IWM, Air Britain, the French, *Aircraft Illustrated, Aviation News,* the late Hermann Göring, Ronald Reagan, Margaret Thatcher and David Steel.

The complexity of the subject can be gauged by the following simple example: most people are happy to refer to the Messerschmitt 109 as that, but to the purist it is just *not* that simple. Let us look at the Bf 109E-7/U-2:

Bf indicates the factory where it was made;
E is the model number;
7 is the series within the model number;
U-2 is a modification added on;

It can go on to define additions as being carried out in the factory or the field... there are no limits.

Be warned that once you embark on this course there is a lot of learning to do but one day when you overhear something like: 'Of course, when they were in the desert 3/JG27 flew Bf 109F-4s with tropical kits, all made by female engineers on the night shift at Augsberg, by pilots selected because of their fair hair, blue eyes, and not one under six foot six inches tall, and everyone had a pair of shoe laces personally donated by Göring...' and understand it, you will know that you are a true Luftwaffe buff and, what's more, halfway towards being a *Real* enthusiast. The other half comes with being able to untangle Japanese aircraft markings, but to do that you must be able to read from left to right as well as up and down at the same time.

Landings

To the enthusiast as well as the casual onlooker, the two most obvious parts of any flight are the take-off and landing. What goes on in between is usually too high to notice. The take-off is more often than not a case of power overcoming gravity, except in notable cases like the C 5

'Why did you say they called this Long John Silver?'

'When we touch down. . . run like hell. . .'

'It's much better to land with the brakes off...'

'I said it handled like a Harrier, NOT landed like a Harrier...'

Galaxy where the curvature of the earth plays a vital role, so to pilots the landing is by far the most important part of the flight. They know this will be viewed with a critical eye by expert and layman alike, and with more than just a passing interest by any passengers there might be on board. The aim is therefore to land the aeroplane delicately and neatly, as near to the end of the runway as possible, leaving enough concrete in front to ensure that it can be stopped before it starts emulating Zola Budd on a cross-country run. In a *Dictionary of Aeronautical Terms*, published in 1943, the two vital elements of any landing, the *run* and the *touch down speed* are quaintly quoted as: 'The distance travelled over the ground by an aerodyne (*sic*) after landing. The speed at which an aeroplane with a normal two-wheel undercarriage stalls when making contact with the ground in the course of a 'three point landing''. Aeroplanes with tricycle undercarriages do not have an exact landing speed, so are flown on to the ground at some speed within a specified range and are stopped by their wheel brakes.'

These days, of course, a two-wheel undercarriage is a rarity so can be discounted, but the statement about tricycle undercarriage aircraft still very much applies. They usually are flown on to or into the ground at *some* speed, as can be illustrated by the Buffalo at the SBAC Display at Farnborough in 1984, and more often than not are successfully stopped by their wheel brakes although on most military airfields there is a net that can be erected to catch those on which the brakes do not prove successful. Around the world navies have solved the problem of landing very much better. Navy pilots just aim their aircraft at the deck of a ship, approach at about 200 knots, then shove down a hook which has six chances of catching a wire stretched across the deck. This stops them from 200 knots per hour to zero in six feet; this why navy pilots can be recognized by their short legs and flattened noses. This could be adopted for all major airports and thus save a lot of space as well as concrete, but it was felt that anything up to 400 passengers arriving unannounced on the flight deck would upset the flight crew's union.

Link Trainer

This will be familiar to the older enthusiast and is mentioned as it might get the preservationists active, in an entirely new and so far unexplored field. It was a small suitcase with stubby wings and a tail, all attached to bellows which moved it in all directions. The victim was totally enclosed. It was supposed to teach instrument flying, but actually caused or cured claustrophobia.

After the Second World War, hundreds of them were buried in a pit in Derbyshire. Recovery could fetch a lot of money, especially in cases where the bellows are still in working order, as they are the same size as bagpipe bags and far more tuneful; ask any U/T (under training) pilot who sat on them for hours.

Today's modern equivalent is called a *Flight Simulator*, often confused by the unitiated with a *Stimulator* which every *Real* enthusiast knows is called a... (Tut! Tut! Bryan, don't known what you mean—Ed.)

Lift

The most vital part of aviation for without it there would be no aeroplanes. Scientifically it is created by air flowing over the aerofoil sections of a wing, but to the *Real* enthusiast it is anything from 35D to 43D or in the most extreme cases small, medium, large, and Samantha Fox! In the context quoted Dolly Parton would be equal to a biplane, and Twiggy an F-104...

'NO he is not madam. . . it's an air conditioner. . .'

'Where's that darn ball-bearing factory?'

'Aircraft calling local control... say AGAIN your position...'

'Yes, the car park is cheaper than landing fees.'

Modellers and Model-making

It may seem odd but it is a fact that even before full-sized aeroplanes flew, people were making models of 'Flying Machines'. Mind you, most of these bore no resemblance to what actually turned out to be genuine aeroplanes, and much the same still applies today in the world of flying model aircraft.

Aircraft modelling is therefore older than aviation itself, and some will argue quite strongly that those who pursue this very enjoyable hobby prove the point. The hobby can be divided into many categories, the two most interesting of which are probably *Flying Models* and *Static Models*. At some time in their life most of the former do, of course, fit into the latter description, these obviously being when they are being constructed and when they are not flying. The most popular of this type is the radio-controlled model. These can be made to scale when they represent miniatures of actual aeroplanes, or semi-scale when they look something like an original, or non-scale, when they usually look like nothing on earth. To the casual observer the object of this part of the hobby appears to be to spend as much money as possible in fitting multi-channel radio equipment to enable the model to be controlled in the air, and as powerful an engine as possible—sometimes on very big models this can be from a lawn mower (an obvious but crafty ploy because if the motor is at 2,000 feet the lawn cannot be cut). The whole assembly, costing several hundreds of pounds, is then sent aloft and can come back to *terra firma* in a most spectacular fashion, making very expensive crunching noises on impact. This usually brings a wry grin (or grimace) from the owner, and cheers all round from spectators.

As interesting as flying models is, it is usually the non-flying scale model that attracts the overall aviation enthusiast, because in this there is a method of turning into three dimensions all the notes, sketches and evidence from

'I think you might get three
more turns on the elastic before
it's too tight Abdul...'

A plastic model enthusiast who
has just discovered that the
REAL DC 3 has twenty more
rivets under the cockpit than
the Airfix model...

photographs and drawings that he has managed to accumulate at all the displays and museums visited during the summer months. What better way to spend a winter evening than whittling wood or pulverizing plastic, until it looks like the latest version of the Tornado or the airliner that took the family to Benidorm. The advent of the plastic construction kit, which started in a small way before the Second World War but came to maturity in the 1950s and '60s, brought this part of the hobby to thousands; and of these there are many hundreds who have become so obsessed that in many cases it is no longer a hobby but close to a religion in which the pursuit of accuracy often leads to the loss of the original objective.

The rot sets in slowly. Most model makers start with a kit of an aeroplane that appeals to them, are quite happy to assemble it with care and paint it carefully. Then they decide to buy a book or magazine devoted to this part of the hobby, and in reading this find that the model they have just made is an eighth of an inch too short. The most popular scale is 1:72 which is six feet to the inch, so it is immediately obvious how *vital* this error is.

This leads to a need to check other documents which might reveal that the shape of the wings is wrong, the tail has too much slope on the leading edge, the cockpit is not rounded enough at the back, the undercarriage is too short and so on. Instead of taking an objective look and thinking, 'It *does* look like the real thing in miniature and Aunty Mary will admire it, and only someone with a micrometer, reference to original drawings and a total obsession with a level of accuracy that is *never* likely to be reached, will notice', the modelmaker throws it away and starts again. He is now on the slippery slope that leads to parts being used from ten different kits, (much to the delight of the manufacturers), to produce one model. He will also become paranoiac with markings, correct colour tints, correct accessories and a hundred and one other minor details that really do not matter. This leads to a great increase in the

quest for more information, which will see more time being spent reading, and compiling questions to ask at next season's Air Shows, that the actual model making takes a back seat. *Real* enthusiasts who reach this stage can be identified by the number of cameras they carry, the number of notebooks and pencils, and the mumbled comments such as, 'Mmmm, I have just measured that Hawk and see that it is two feet longer than the Airbox kit says. Now, if I can get British Aerospace to re-jig it, I shall not need to buy five Airbox and one Matchfix model to construct an accurate fuselage.' They will also be observed in groups discussing how many proportions of Light Gull Grey to mix with Dull Sea Grey to get Barley Grey to BS 381, and arguing that 74 Squadron must have their Phantoms painted the wrong colours, because *that* one over there is nothing like *Scale Models* or *Airfix Magazine* says it should be.

So there you have it, briefly but to the point. *You* too can become a *Real* modeller but to do so you must become a *Real* enthusiast first, and the only way to do that is to read every possible book and magazine on the subject; but be warned, it can be very damaging to your true enjoyment of what can otherwise be a fascinating hobby.

Memorabilia

Like modelmaking, the collecting of bits and pieces
connected with aviation can become an obsession leading in
the end to a total oversight as to what the original objective
was. If you start looking for so called 'Collectors' Items', be
wary of the following:

There is enough original fabric on offer from von
Richthofen's Fokker Triplane to cover *all* triplanes ever
built;

There were over 30,000 Messerschmitt Bf 109s built, so the
chances of the part you are now being offered as coming off
the one flown by Adolf Galland during the Battle of Britain
is fairly remote;

Military pilots' cape leather gloves have 'PORT' and

'It's only JUST below the 3 mm minimum.'

'STBD' marked on the fingers, *not* 'LEFT' and 'RGHT';
these are civil airline pilots' gloves (See also under
Concorde);
Shares in Westland are *not* that easy to come by;
There are *no* secret hideaways where twenty Spitfires have
been found still in their crates.

  If you want to collect aviation trivia, stick to those that
you can verify such as:
Pieces from tyres burst by the Red Arrows. These are
plentiful and at this time not worth a great deal on the
second-hand market. . .
Hermann Göring's back collar stud. He wore a clean shirt
every day and always insisted on a new set of studs, so these
too are plentiful and can be identified by their shape, which
is a cross when viewed from the side. . .
Most Ministers of Defence's knowledge of aeronautical
strategy and tactics. Usually very similar to a blank exercise
book bought in most large stationery shops. . .

'It's OK. . . I always leave the finer detail to the back seat driver.'

The autographs of most aviation journalists: start with those listed in the appropriate section. Good hunting!

Museums

When the Multi-Role Combat Aircraft (MRCA) was first being designed and before it became the Tornado, a German engineer involved with the project was asked on British television why the design team had opted for variable sweep wings. He replied, 'Beecaws ven der machinen ist reddy to go into die servees mit der Luftwaffen, das vingens will be able to be sweeped backen zo der maschinen vill fitten into das museum'.

This statement not only indicates how long it takes to get a modern military combat aircraft from the design stage into service, but also how the requirements of future historians are catered for, since variable sweep wings have proved virtually useless for almost every other task they were designed for.

There are more aviation museums per square mile in every country of the world than there are any other type of similar establishment. They range from the large impressive government or public subscription-funded ones, to layouts of twisted metal displayed in anything from a grotty garage to a leaking lean-to. Some have well looked-after collections of all types of aeroplanes, whilst others have cast-off cut-outs from film sets and rows and rows of poorly made models and a few dusty paintings. Most enthusiasts quickly get to know those that are worth driving hundreds of miles to visit, but there are some who regard any collection, however modest, worthy of taking a look at. The majority of *Real* enthusiasts often bemoan the fact that there are few of what they call 'Flying Museums', but these are people who clearly have no knowledge of aerodynamics or architecture, since it should be obvious to even the most dedicated that it is not possible to fit wings or engines to

massive buildings and make them fly. Howard Hughes
proved this with his 'Spruce Goose', and Bristol as well as
Saunders-Roe came close with the Brabazon and Princess
Flying Boat respectively.

Man-Powered Flight

Despite adequate proof by Icarus and many other early
pioneers, there are those who still pursue this impossible
dream. It is not strictly true to say that it is totally
impossible, since governments—looking at ways of cutting
back on aviation expenditure whilst making pilots work for a
living—have over the years offered cash incentives to
inventors. The most famous prize is probably that put up by
the industrialist Henry Kremer, who for his somewhat
modest (by modern standards) investment has been treated
to years of fun by those trying to pedal their way into the
air. Pedal power has proved to be the most successful but
attempts to get 400 people in a Boeing 747 all pushing pedals

'Any more defence cuts and NATO might just as well call it a day.'

in unison and at the right speed as well as consistently for eight-hour periods, have proved impossible.

It is rumoured that many years ago the pioneer inventor Sir George Cayley did frighten his footman into propelling one of his man-powered aircraft which he had christened *Cayley's Comet* into orbit at such a speed that it now only comes back every 76 years, but present day historians dispute this story and say that confusion has arisen over the exodus into space during the late 'fifties of a rock 'n roll star known as Bill Haley... the truth as any *Real* enthusiast will tell you, is that it was a man called Bailey, who still refuses to come home. Maybe Mr Kremer has the answer.

For those interested the Kremer prize has still not been totally claimed, so for those readers who get themselves into a *flap* at the least provocation, this is a field of aviation that could still bring worthwhile rewards.

Military Aviation

This attracts a much greater following than any other part of the world of aviation; which is strange when the number of civil airliners, airports, flying clubs and general availability of all related material is considered. Perhaps it is the challenge to the *Real* enthusiast to find out as much as he can about things he shouldn't then talk authoritatively to those who in most cases don't care about the subject, know even less about it, and wonder what on earth he is talking about.

Military aircraft come in so many shapes and sizes, have so many extras added to them, are coded with such a bewildering array of numbers and letters, that they enable anyone who is prepared to devote a little time to the subject to become a much-quoted expert. Before embarking on this interesting but tortuous route you must carry out the following exercise:

Re-read the entry under Luftwaffe as this unveils the tip of the iceberg...

Look at your bank balance, because you will need to buy *Jane's* every year (currently about £75.00 a copy) and all magazines with a military bent...

Do a crash course in Japanese, since their magazines are usually the most authoritative...

Visit *every* air show, except those at Shuttleworth...

Buy a full set of camping gear unless of course you can afford to stay at hotels or guest houses...

Learn by heart the location of every military airfield in the country and the best viewing area...

Alternatives to the above are:

Learn first-aid and join the St John Ambulance Brigade...

Become a civilian instructor with the Air Training Corps or join the Royal Observer Corps...

Get a part-time job as hamburger salesman...

all these carry the perk of getting you into air shows for nothing.

If you are really desperate, become an air correspondent, a volunteer member of any Air Show organizing committee,

or buy an exotic military aircraft and be paid to take it to air shows. . . but whatever you do, *never, never* enlist, for the armed Services are the last places where you can expect to become an expert on anything, let alone aviation.

Finally, if you are still keen, just remember one of the definitions of the word 'Expert': If you turn a tap fully on the water will *spurt* out, turn it off quickly and the tap will drip. . . so an ex-spurt is nothing more than a. . .

Mach Number

The speed of sound changes with variations in temperature and altitude, but is generally accepted to be around 760 mph at sea level and 660 mph at 36,000 feet, above which temperature and therefore speed of sound remain constant. It was felt that pilots needed some warning as their aircraft approached the speed of sound, so although the banging, buffeting and occasional popping out of rivets gave good aural warning, a visual indication on the instrument panel was felt to be worth including. Dr Ernst Mach, an Austrian physicist, had related the angle of shock wave of a bullet to the velocity of sound and gave it a constant factor, and it was decided to use this to relate the airspeed to the true local speed of sound. Therefore Mach 1 represents the speed of sound at any altitude and higher or lower numbers are a percentage of this speed; for example Mach .75 is 75 per cent and Mach 2, twice the speed of sound. Enough of these technicalities, it is just sufficient to ponder how fortunate we are that the good Doctor had such a suitable name: suppose it had been Dr Smith who had thought it out; it would not be very exciting to say, 'I have flown at Smith 2 on the Concorde', would it?

Think also how difficult it might have been if it had been Dr Culpepper-Hidlegate, or if Beethoven had been a physicist, his fifth would have a real boom, or if Schubert had tried we could have an unfinished speed of sound. Or if Dr Mach had been a composer, we might have had the flight of the bumble bee on a Mach 5 Steinway. This is an interesting game to play whilst waiting in the departure lounge, or for your turn in 'Trivial Pursuit'. Whatever funny or suitable names you might come up with, we are stuck with a Machmeter in the cockpit to give visual indication that the aeroplane is flying very fast. Low down in a fast aeroplane, if the pilot looks out and the telegraph poles look like a continuous fence, he knows he is travelling *very* fast and can safely ignore any flashing blue lights in his rear-view mirror.

Navigators

'It's OK navigator. . . there's the AA building, they will give us a check route.'

There is a love/hate relationship between pilots and navigators; they each love to hate the other. This is not really true but is part of the folklore that has been allowed to grow around aircrew, especially those in the armed Services. Pilots will often refer to navigators as 'ballast' and navigators to pilots as 'drivers'. Either expression is likely to cause considerable annoyance to the recipient. Pilots will also often refer to small portions of a delicacy, say caviar, as 'Navigator's Brains', while navigators will retaliate by referring to an empty plate as 'Pilot's Brains'.

But beware! It is unwise for those on the outside to assume either mantle lightly, since any member of an aircrew will immediately join forces with a colleague to fend off an interloper. Both pilots and navigators will often call air electronic operators 'ballast', that is until they want a fuse changed or any electrical gadget repaired. *All* aircrew will refer to any ground crew officer as 'A Penguin' or a 'Wingless Wonder'. Whatever else you may have read it is not true to say that navigators are failed pilots. . . that is,

unless you want to bring a quick end to your *Real* enthusiast status.

Just remember a navigator will be lost with a map of the London Underground, unless he has a pilot to guide him...

At air shows you will recognise any aircrew member who is not wearing flying kit, by the small scars around his mouth where he has been receiving lessons in eating with a fork.

Naval Aviation

The Navy gave up all claims to aviation when the Royal Naval Air Service became amalgamated with the Royal Flying Corps on 1 April 1918, to form the Royal Air Force. Since then they have been allowed to have some older type aeroplanes which they flew from flat decks on ships they called aircraft carriers. Although they had some degree of success, the fact that anyone was prepared to leave what was virtually their airfield, and let it sail around all over the place

'My bloody winchman never wants to get up these days.'

Due to defence cuts in the FAA there was a time when fuel was saved by aerial towing.

whilst they flew in many other directions, really says it all.

Eventually all aircraft carriers were scrapped and the Navy was allowed to have a few helicopters. The Harrier was also given to them since this can be made to act like a helicopter: to keep some of the older 'salts' happy, smaller carriers were provided.

Oddly enough, most other nations still persist with bigger and bigger aircraft carriers, carrying faster and faster aeroplanes. This just underlines how advanced the military thinking of the British is when compared with other countries, who have not yet appreciated that it is very much more economical to try to make all Naval pilots expert at landing on any flat deck or even a cargo lashed to the deck of a freighter and get the Captain to take you wherever he is going at no cost in aircraft fuel to the taxpayer: not to mention a free cruise in the sun for the pilot. So the slogan 'Fly Navy' often seen displayed in many places, can have two distinct meanings, depending how you interpret the first word.

Non-Induced Drag

This is an impromptu act put on at an aircrew party by a female impersonator or a member of the womens' services... there is in fact often little recognisable difference between the two.

Nimbo-Stratus *(Abb. Nimbus)*

The winner of the 1956 Derby at Epsom. Its connection with aviation is that it was trailing by ten lengths five furlongs from home, when a low flying Meteor put the fear of God into it. Despite an objection and Steward's Enquiry, the horse was placed first and the Meteor disqualified as it was overweight; not an unusual situation for a Meteor.

Nimrod *(see also Books)*

'Once upon a time when they went to the big happy hunting ground in the sky, all Comet airliners became Nimrods. One day a wooden mock-up that was called Nimrod AEW 3 told so many tall stories to those who were building it that its nose grew and grew and grew. It was eventually made with a very large nose and tail to match and those who had believed its stories were all taken for a long and unprofitable ride on a secret radar set that didn't exist. But a Fairey (*sic*) Princess called AWACS came all the way from America to rescue the poor unfortunate people who had believed the wicked Nimrod AEW 3. AWACS chased off the naughty secret radar and turned its hiding space in Nimrod AEW 3 into passenger space for *Real* aviation enthusiasts who wanted to go on day trips to all sorts of air shows. So everyone lived happily ever after and the AWACS and its friend in America laughed all the way to the bank.'

When it was found that the British-designed radar for the AEW 3 Nimrod wouldn't work, all the spare space was used as a flying wardrobe on Royal Tours. This stopped the taxpayers' money being a total waste.

Ornithopter

Since man became obsessed with flight he has tried to copy the birds, and many attempts have been made to produce a machine that flies, just like a bird, by flapping its wings. Needless to say these have all failed, although some have come close, and nature still remains the only successful designer. Never willing to admit defeat man has looked at birds in connection with other spheres of aviation, and there are notable examples of efforts to cover aircraft with feathers to try to develop perfect camouflage. The Peruvian Air Force was fairly successful but kept having its feathered-covered aircraft abducted by the Greater Crested Eagle which lives in that country. The only recorded attempt in the western world failed when a squadron of Hunters that were camouflaged with feathers, persisted in heading south when winter came despite every effort by the pilots to stop them. This brought the experiment to a swift end.

Some notable aircraft that have flown with flapping wings, although these were not designed to be the motive power, are:

the Fw 200,
Wellesley,
Zlin, B-47,
B-52,
all Tupolev bombers,
hang gliders,
and the C-5B Galaxy.

Wellington,
Olympia 419,
Boeing 707,
U-2,
all man-powered aircraft,
most micro-lights

Oxygen

Aircrew started a rumour that it is essential to breathe this gas above 10,000 feet otherwise you turn blue. There are no blue airline passengers (except those travelling to political conferences), so it can be dismissed as purely propaganda, because it happens to be the best substance for clearing hangovers.

123

Observer Corps

Now of course known as the Royal Observer Corps, this fine body of men and women can trace its origin to the days before RADAR when its members were the eyes and ears of the country. They were all experts at aircraft recognition and during the war lived in establishments called 'Posts' where from open towers they observed the heavens and reported anything that moved. Below the observation tower was a plotting room where all movements were recorded and reported to central command where they were acted upon. Many members now happily recall those days by producing all types of documents issued by many different authorities showing, among other things, colours aircraft would be painted, special things to look for, unusual shapes and so on. In fact most enthusiasts know that during the war *all* aircraft were painted black, as this is proved by the drawings displayed in Observer Corps' Headquarters.

Many members perfected the identification of aircraft by sound. The advent of the jet brought this to a premature end following an incident in 1945 when the Little Hampton and Bognor Post reported a Vampire approaching in thick cloud and this turned out to be the post cleaner's Electrolux cylinder vacuum cleaner, which had seen better days, being used in the room below. The speed of jets also put recognition and reporting beyond most observers, so today they carry out an equally important task in reporting nuclear fall-out, and will therefore be the first to know when we are all dead following a nuclear attack.

Pilots

Enough has been written under other headings for the tyro to understand what he should and shouldn't know about pilots, it is perhaps sufficient to sum up with the following *aide memoire*:

Pilots are drivers operating in three dimensions, and even if they do wear 'Y'-fronts on the outside of their trousers they are not supermen;

Most of them are colour blind, which is why all routes are marked Red 1, Green 4, Blue 3, etc;

They can all tell better stories than can be heard on 'Jackanory';

The very best ones are usually called 'George';

Most have an enormous capacity for beer, except when flying, when they stick to fruit juice or Alka Seltzer;

All of them love navigators...

'This is your captain speaking... we are just passing over Paris, and to the left you will see that the FT index has fallen... sorry I'll say that again.'

Propellers

These are oddly-shaped pieces of wood or metal fitted to the fronts of older aeroplanes. They are much loved by collectors who will travel miles to look at or even buy a wooden one with a clock in the middle. How anyone ever told the time when these clocks were rotating so fast is one of the many unsolved mysteries of the world of aviation. Most such propellers when displayed above mantlepieces in homes, bars or flying clubs are reputed to have come from: Sopwith Camels, Hawker Harts, Spitfires, Messerschmitt Bf 109s, Hurricanes or Pitts Specials.

Unfortunately it is hard to prove to the owners that there were not that many aircraft in the category claimed, or they didn't have wooden two-bladed propellers; so it is best to just agree. The only known case where the source of such a memento can be disputed is in the club room of the 'Flying Leprechaun' at Dublin Airport, where their clock propeller carries a brass plate stating that it came from the prototype Concorde.

Examples of metal propellers with very bent tips, and no clocks, usually come from aircraft in which the pilot landed without his gear down, the crew abandoned it for reasons best known to themselves, or a short-sighted airman drove over it on a tractor. However, all these will be shown as coming from a Lancaster, Halifax, B-17 or, if very rare, the Bf 110 Hess flew to Scotland.

Paintings

Collecting paintings and prints has become very much an integral part of the aviation enthusiast's way of life. Many have also taken up the palette and brush, cut off one of their ears, and had a go themselves. Original works of art with aviation subjects can be very expensive, so the majority tend to stay with prints, most of which are signed by the artist or one of the subjects featured in the painting. These can have a remarkable habit of increasing in value overnight if the subject matter happens to pass on.

So, if you are a pilot or member of the crew of an aeroplane that has achieved some historical landmark, and you are asked to sign a limited edition print depicting the event, just be a little wary.

As in most things there are those out to make the quick buck so beware of anyone who tries to sell a: Renoir of the Dams Raid, an original Picasso of 'Vapour Trails over London', or an impressionist painting of a multi-coloured Phantom alleged to have been executed by Wilf Hardy whilst he was laying on his back in a hangar at Boscombe Down.

Publications

Aviation periodicals, journals, magazines, and newspapers are a minefield for the unwary; it has to be very much a case of 'you pays your money and takes your chance'. Some have very strong political inclinations which can be quickly detected in the editorial, some have a holier-than-thou attitude, which is hard to detect unless you happen to be in a situation where you are handling press pass applications. In this case it becomes very easy to detect *all* types of publications and their staff, and is perhaps the best vantage point from which to take this short look.

Some well established monthlies feel it is a God-given right for them to have twice as many passes as any other, this is probably because their standard of writing and journalism is so poor that the editor needs as many reports as he can get to produce one that may be fairly accurate.

Some magazines concentrate on modern aviation, others vintage, others on events, others on aircraft ancient and modern, some on the world-wide scene, and yet others on every possible facet. Very few succeed in covering all they set out to with any great success, and if you select what appeals to you, and stick with it, you will eventually find that it will cover everything; for there is only one basic subject and eventually all that is written is regurgitated and will appear in most magazines over a period of time. Those just reporting Bèriot's cross-Channel flight are obviously well out of touch and should be avoided.

Another thing to look for is the quality of printing and photographic reproduction. These days there are many magazines with special editions, supplements, colour inserts and so on, all carrying high cover prices for colour pictures that would be just as informative in black and white. There are, of course, many produced on paper that is one stage off being pulp, with photographs processed in mulligatawny soup.

There is also a wide range of so-called enthusiast publications which are often no more than sheets of duplicated paper run-off on a second-hand duplicator with leaky rollers, and photographs that look like Belisha's original drawings for his pedestrian crossing. Most of these are produced by 'Groups' who have discovered that some airshow organizers will give Press Passes to anyone claiming to produce a magazine. Over a period of one Air Show season, the outlay on a few sheets of headed paper, from their local quick-print shop, a second-hand duplicator bought off the WI and a ream or two of paper, will be recovered in free admission tickets.

The only advice is to do what most other people do, that is to visit the local multi-national newsagents on a Saturday, and read *all* the aviation magazines. This should be done by placing your chosen reading material between the covers of *Mayfair, Penthouse, Fiesta* or *Forum*, otherwise people looking over your shoulder will think you are some kind of pervert.

Preservation Groups

Discover something old or interesting and a Group will be

set up to preserve or renovate it. As commendable as this might be, the problem comes in defining what is *worth* preserving or renovating, and this applies more in the field of aviation than any other, except perhaps automobiles.

Most aviation groups will give an infinite number of reasons why someone—usually the mythical *they* who accept the blame for everything—should have had the foresight to preserve:

Every biplane that ever flew;

A sample of every bomber or fighter that saw action in either World War;

Flying examples of every trainer used by the RAF;

All Sunderland flying boats;

Guy Gibson's batman;

The remains of von Richthofen's Fokker Triplane;

The Wright brothers' shoe laces;

The pen Harold Wilson used to cancel the TSR2 contract;

The TSR2 jigs;

Every mark of Shackleton; or

Flying versions of all Canberras.

The list is endless and reading through the columns of the various Preservation Group publications (most of which fit into the category of enthusiast publications) you will find that there are endless tales of crates of complete Lancasters, Hampdens, Defiants, or whatever happens to be in vogue at the time, found under tons of scrap in breakers' yards in the Midlands. If any of these are ever recovered is hard to say, but is very unlikely otherwise every Group would have its own historic airframe to preserve, rebuild or fawn over.

Of course most of the Groups are very sincere and quite harmless, and one has to admire their tenacity and sincerity in overcoming such overwhelming misunderstanding from so many Air Show organizers and museum curators. Membership can be very rewarding, but like modelmaking, it is too easy to become obsessed, and the convert can soon find himself involved in compiling thousands of useless statistics such as how many shoe laces were lost in the

Falklands, to the number of half-inch pop rivets in a Lancaster tailplane, to the serial of every type of aircraft that has crashed in the Himalayas on a Good Friday. All of this will be set on a home computer, bound between two sheets of cardboard and sold to other enthusiasts for sums ranging from a few pence to over £20.00.

All, however, form a part of the rich tapestry of the world of the aviation enthusiast, and our intentions are to guide— not to recommend or condemn. (NB, any Group recommending this book will be advised under cover of a plain envelope, of the whereabouts of two brand new Fairey Battles, still in their crates, concealed on 10 May 1940 in France.)

Pterodactyl

An aeroplane designed to save expenditure by omitting the tail. Some examples did fly but the experiment was abandoned when housewives donated enough saucepans to provide tails for all aeroplanes that needed them.

Quotations

Throughout the history of aviation there have been many famous quotations, and just a few examples of those that can be repeated are given; there are many, many more:

'I can see no practical military use for the aeroplane.' Orville Wright.

'There is no future for manned military aircraft...' Duncan Sandys, 1957.

'Night-fighting will never happen.' Hermann Göring, 1939.

'I think it most unlikely that aeronautics will ever be able to exercise a decisive influence on travel. Man is not an albatross...' H.G. Wells, 1901.

'They'll never do it. It is only given to God and angels to fly...' Bishop Wright (father of Orville Wright), 1903.

'It is a bluff my dear Ernst. They can make cars and refrigerators but not aircraft.' Hermann Göring, 1941 (Speaking to Milch about America's aircraft production).

'Man will never set foot on the moon...' Sir Harold Spencer Jones (Astronomer Royal), 1957.

'If an enemy bomber reaches the Ruhr, my name is not Hermann Göring... You can call me Meier.' Hermann Göring, 1940.

'When in doubt, mumble. When in trouble, delegate.' RAF Staff College.

'Anything that can go wrong, will go wrong'. Pilot Officer Percy Prune.

'If it jams—force it. If it breaks it needed replacing anyway.' A/C 2 Plonk.

Red Arrows

The RAF's premier aerobatic team which was 21 years old in 1986. Descended from the Yellow Jacks but after confusion with AA lifting gear, changed its name to that now used. Team consists of ten former navigators who fly together so they do not get lost.

The flying display is done by nine while the tenth checks on the quickest route by following rail or motorway systems to the next engagement. Bad weather is used as an excuse to cancel displays, but is often because road or railway cannot be seen. Due to MoD cuts in expenditure, the team will soon consist of one aircraft, towing eight glass fibre one-to-one replicas. The latter are already under test by RAF recruiting units, and introduction will be delayed only for as long as it takes to find a pilot able to navigate successfully by himself. As part of the Public Relations programme, pilots of the Red Arrows are encouraged to answer questions from the public at air displays, and the following is a guide to what and what *not* to ask:

Red Leader to Arrows: 'We'll try shaking him off with a Diamond Nine loop.'

'We must stop meeting like this.'

Questions to ask
Can I have your autograph?

How do you keep so cool
and calm?

Why do you think you are so
much better than other
teams?

It must be very hard to fly a
Hawk?

Can I see you after the
show? (Only ask this if you
are a female.)

Are you an Air Vice
Marshal?

How can you see through all
that smoke?

Questions not to ask
Are you any good at mending
punctures?

Is the Airfix model of the
Hawk accurate?

Do you *all* have shares in
Dunlop?

My Dad says the
Thunderbirds fly faster. Do
they?

What is the co-efficient of
aerodynamic penetration of
the Hawk?

Is it true that all Red Arrows
pilots have a AVM in the
family?

RAF

It is expensive (very) to learn to fly or to be trained as a mechanic but Her Majesty the Queen owns the largest number of aeroplanes in Great Britain and if you talk nicely to the gentlemen in recruiting offices they might be persuaded to have a few words with her, and providing you do not work for 'Spitting Image', she might well decide to let you learn on one of her aeroplanes. If so, you will become a member of the biggest flying club in England, and whilst you might not fly as often as some of the Private Flying Clubs, you will get a free suit to wear and a very nice tie that can be worn after duty.

If you happen to be American, when reading the above substitute The President in place of HM The Queen. Have a nice day.

'Before we go ahead with this lynching, shouldn't there be a court of enquiry or something?'

RIB

The wings of *all* aeroplanes have Ribs which stop the top
surfaces hitting bottom surfaces. They were given this name
to commemorate the first lady aviation enthusiast who made
her maiden flight by trying to pinch one of her husband's rib
bones but woke him up in the process; his well placed foot
did the rest...

RADAR

This is a very complex subject, but it is sufficient to know
that big wire mesh dish-shaped aerials that revolve all round
airfields are to receive satellite TV pictures from America so
that air traffic controllers keep ahead of the rest of the
population in viewing American soap operas. This
equipment should *not* be confused with RADA which is
where all pilots, police dogs, British Airways cabin staff and
air show organizers are trained.

Retired Aviators

Usually recognized by long flowing white or grey (To BS
381c) moustache which measures at least 200 mm from tip to
tip. They should be engaged in conversation only if you have
several hours to spare. Usually very good sources of
information, but this must be checked most carefully as they
tend to become confused over where and when they flew, the
type of aircraft and whose side the Italians were on. When
conversation reaches the point where their eyes glaze over
and they start with '...and there I was upside down...' it is
time to find another pub.

Most of them spend their time reading the 'Help' and
'Where are they now' columns in *Air Mail*, hoping that:
'The red headed WAAF from billet 5 RAF Benbecula, 1943
seeks her popsie wopsie from No 51 Sqn.'
...or:

'Would "Ginger" Lane who knew Ronnie Simpkins, a WOP/AG on Halifaxes of 9 Sqn, please contact Fred Rumbelow who is writing a book about the installation of the Elsan in WW2 bombers.'
. . . do not receive any replies to their requests.

Spotters

'Now look mam, I aint been aparked just here for more than ten minutes.'

Spotting is nearly as old as aviation itself, although the activities of a certain group of ladies in 1985 in 'spotting' a so-called spy plane with white paint at an Air Show, should not be confused with the real thing. The art of spotting was originally the ability to recognize any aeroplane almost instantly. This was called aircraft recognition and was usually done by members of the Royal Observer Corps who practised with a *Flash Trainer*, often operated by a member in a dirty fawn-coloured raincoat. The word is now more commonly associated with enthusiasts who make lists of aircraft types they have seen and keep records of them by

serial numbers and/or civil registrations. Some of these have been touched on under Civil Aviation. Most spotters spend a lot of time writing letters to magazines which may have quite innocently mentioned an aircraft by its number. Their letters are a skilled art and usually look something like this:
'Dear Sir,

'I notice on page 32 of your otherwise most excellent publication a glaring error relating to the Sopwith Camel flown by 2nd Lt Ronald Nearmis-Sternpost (Michael Caine) in the film *Wings Over The East End*. This was *not* the original *R5132*, currently on display in the IWM, but a replica made from the wings of Stampe *G-RAVE,* the fuselage of Tiger Moth *G-NONE*, and components from the Aerospatiale prototype Jaguar.
'The original is, of course, believed to have seen a lot of action over the Somme and would not be allowed to be taken from the hallowed halls of the IWM. (Quite rightly so.) However, full credit must be given to those concerned in making the replica so life-like, since this contributed more to the aviation authenticity of the film, which was only spoiled by Michael Caine wearing Mk VIII goggles and a Bone Dome (!) in the scene where he found the heroine drinking his gin and swallowing large quantities of paracetamol when she thought he had been shot down by Count von Pooroften. Incidentally, his Fokker Dr 1 Triplane was borrowed from the current front-line defence of Cork squadron of the Irish Air Corps.' . . . and so on.
Others are much more to the point:
'Dear Sir,

'The Harrier captioned as *XV718* on page 18 of your June edition couldn't have been, as this aircraft was scrapped after a heavy landing in Fakenham High Street on 1 April 1984. (The parking ticket was cancelled after intervention by the Prime Minister.)'

It is not so much the spotting that makes this part of the hobby difficult, but the letter-writing.

Stall

Officially this is when an aeroplane falls out of the sky due to insufficient forward speed to maintain lift. Unofficially it is a ploy used by Spotters when they are moved on from areas where they shouldn't be, or the habitat of such enthusiasts when they are not trying to get into areas where they shouldn't be.

Stars

Heavenly bodies used by aircrew to navigate by when all else fails. Some well-known ones are: Sirius, Canopus, Rigel Kent (no relation to Bruce), Vega, Archernar (no relation to Dan), Joan Collins, Selina Scott, Samantha Fox and Patrick Moore.

To keep aircrew up-to-date additions are published every day on page three of the *Sun* and monthly in such guides to

Once you get a Press Pass, ALL the fun goes out of air displays...

the galaxy as *Mayfair, Penthouse* and *Playboy*. Aircrew
always regard this part of their knowledge as extremely vital
which is proved by extracts from the journals quoted, being
prominently displayed in crew rooms throughout the world.

Southerly Burster

Actually a line-squall in east or south-east Australia; but
more commonly known as Dolly Parton.

Societies

This is another area where great caution must be exercised.
There are many professional societies which are all dedicated
to the furtherance or study of aviation, and these *must not*
be confused with those that are up-market enthusiast groups
calling themselves Societies to achieve a 'higher' standing.
Like Groups they publish newsletters which vary in quality
of print and content, but in the main are different because
they try to introduce 'political' comment which can be
hobby horses of the President, Chairman, Treasurer,
Secretary, Membership Secretary or Editor; in many cases
these will all be the same person.

Among the aviation news, which will be slanted towards
the aim of the particular society concerned, will be found
such gems as (in plastic modelling Society magazines) the
President's views of those who use material other than
plastic, the members' views of the competition secretary
(especially if they didn't win the last competition) and
denials from the Editor that he is responsible for the
content. All highly amusing, but not guaranteed to increase
their standing in the eyes of potential members or those to
whom application might be made for press passes or other
perks.

The aims and objectives of most of these fringe societies

Overseas members of the 'Build a Lysander Lookalike Society' on their annual trip to Shuttleworth.

can be identified by their titles, many of which are based on geographical locations:

BABBS. The Beccles & Bungay Beaufighter Society. Formed to commemorate the part played by the ladies of the area in knitting socks for Beaufighter crews. Both members meet every third Tuesday in 'The Bull'.

CLOTS. Crewe Lancaster Operations v Trains Society. Dedicated to trips flown by Lancaster crews against European railway systems (not post-war). All six members, plus two dogs, meet in the waiting room of Crewe station (by permission of BR).

There are Societies devoted to just about everything connected with aviation. In the main they are quite harmless, and if you have a tie and jacket you can attend their meetings, but in the main they should not be taken as seriously as they take themselves!

Stickers

These are a comparatively new innovation in the world of aviation but have become very much sought-after by collectors, and are a useful form of 'currency' at Air Shows. Small quantities are produced by Service units, Groups and Societies, and these are the most valuable. It is considered funny to 'zap' aircraft and buildings with them, providing you are not caught, especially if the sticker happens to read 'Toilet' and you are putting it on the inside of the entry door of an airliner.

It is also not good taste to put 'Re-cycled Tornado' on a Shuttleworth Collection Avro 504K, or 'Lancs Rule OK!' on the B-17 *Sally-B*, or any B-17 if it comes to that.

Spitfire

More has been written about the Spitfire than any other British World War 2 aircraft, but the truth can now be told.

There was in fact only *one* Spitfire, which flew on 5 March 1936 (true despite attempts by authors cashing-in on the 50th anniversary by stating they were laying a legend by claiming it was 6 March), but it was photographed from 24 different angles on over 27,000 occasions, sometimes against a background of the ocean when it was captioned Seafire.

All the battle scenes shown on film and TV are fakes using cardboard cut-outs and replicas made from aluminium saucepans and frying pans.

The story that the Luftwaffe Ace Adolf Galland asked for a squadron of Spitfires in 1940 has been totally misunderstood. When Göring asked him what he wanted he said, 'Ein vorsitz bei Speichel Feuer!', which is 'A seat by a spitting fire' (it was a cold summer), and not 'Forty flippin' Spitfires', as is generally believed. The truth is that the translating 'bug' used by GCHQ at that time had not been Union-approved and was of very poor quality. But the legend was allowed to grow as it did wonders for morale.

Flying Spitfires seen today are in fact one-to-one replicas of the original made from plastic under a Government scheme to increase employment in the Private Sector.

To put the record straight, there were over five million Hurricanes made and some of these were called Spitfires by a Hawker PR man who had been fired by Vickers Supermarine when he asked why they were using Heinkel 70 wings... but that's another story.

Stressed Skin

An external skin carrying part or all of the main loads of an airframe; now we're back to page three and *Mayfair*.

Sesquiplane

An unusual type of aeroplane developed by the Scottish Division of Armstrong Whitworth when they were looking to save money. A.V. MacRoe-MacRoe hit upon the idea of fitting half-size wings as the bottom planes of a biplane. He didn't quite have the nerve to go the whole way and delete the whole wing. But cutting costs on bottom wings by half, saved a lot of money. The name was derived when the Chief Accountant stopped counting the savings and pronounced, 'What a sexy wee plane'. Over the years this became a sesquiplane. Most notable example is the Siskin, a good modern example is the F-104.

Slang

There is much use of slang in the world of aviation, most of it deriving from Service sources. Some of the following are typical and can 'date' the user who will often be found to have no experience of life in one of the flying Services:

Gone for a Burton.	Means to have been killed, disappeared or demobbed. Originated from getting a suit from the well-known tailor.
Blood Wagon.	Ambulance.
Popsie.	Girl friend,
Pongo.	Army officer.
Fish-Heads.	Royal Navy personnel.
Sprog.	New recruit.
Prang (very dated).	Air crash.
Snowdrop.	RAF Policeman.
Wingless Wonders.	Ground staff.
Penguin.	RAF Officer without flying badge.
Gen.	Information. Often used with 'pukka', when it means good, or 'duff' when it means bad.
Stuffed cloud.	Low cloud surrounding high ground.
Waterborne cowboy.	Alternative for Navy flyer.
WAFU.	Member of the Fleet Air Arm.
Line-shoot.	Unlikely and exaggerated story.
Line-book.	Kept on most Squadrons to record above.
Erk.	Any airman below NCO rank.
Rock ape.	Any member of the RAF Regiment.
Air Commode.	Air Commodore.
Station Master.	Officer Commanding any RAF Station.
Driver (airframe).	Pilot.
Gone for a ball of chalk.	Killed or something that has gone wrong in every possible way.
Bang seat.	Ejection seat.

Travel (Air)

Travel by air is something everyone enjoys. Once each year everyone, however rich or poor, has a free trip around the sun. Air travel is now so common that everyone is used to it, and happily accepts that it takes twice as long to get to the airport and go through all the formalities as it does to fly to most places in the world, but on long flights it is worth it just to see old movies. A word of warning, never try to equate air fares with distance travelled, otherwise you will either go mad or get a distorted view of the geography of the world. For example, it is possible to fly almost anywhere in the USA for about $50, but will cost you about $450 to get to the USA in the first place. Similarly the fare from Heathrow to Paris is £200 but to Toronto it is £215 (1986 prices).

Ties

In the same way that it is the 'done thing' to wear the correct tie at Lords, Henley and Wimbledon, it is also considered good etiquette to wear the right tie to aviation functions.

Always	*Never*
For flying displays and Air Shows:	
Any RAF or Squadron.	Royal Fleet Auxiliary.
Fleet Air Arm.	Merchant Navy.
Private Flying Club.	Old Merchant Taylors.
Royal Aeronautical Society.	Eton.
Royal Aero Club	Harrow
Army Air Corps.	RCT
Glider Pilot Regiment.	Brigade of Guards.
Any bow tie.	IPMS.
Caterpiller Club.	MCC.
RFC.	CND.
For RAF Museums:	
Any of above except Army Air Corps, Glider Pilot Regiment or Fleet Air Arm.	Any of the above and REME. Household Cavalry.

He was wearing WHAT tie!!!!!?

For Army Museums:

None of the above except Army Air Corps, Glider Pilot Regiment and Fleet Air Arm.

Any of the above except CND.

For Fleet Air Arm Museum:

None of the above except Fleet Air Arm.

None of the above except Royal Fleet Auxiliary and Merchant Navy.

When visiting Shuttleworth:

No tie but a cravat with a paisley pattern but strictly nothing with jet engine or swept wing motif.

Any enthusiast museum or collection:

Open necked shirt only, but any tie can be used to support trousers, or if really upmarket, use a pair of matching ties instead of hairy string tied just below knees of corduroy trousers but *not* jeans.

NB. The publishers and author cannot accept any responsibility if you are refused admission for wearing the wrong tie. The above is a general guide only, and it is always wise to check with the organizers before setting out.

Talks

A lot of information can be gathered by attending talks and listening hard. It is best to avoid those of a very high technical content which includes many presented by members of the Royal Aeronautical Society, unless of course you want to catch up on some lost sleep in an atmosphere of total relaxation broken only by the soft droning of the presenter.

Enthusiast Groups, Societies and Clubs are noted for their lively presentations, which they usually call planning meetings for the coming season or Annual General Meetings; don't risk the latter unless you want to get on the committee. Lists are usually published in most aviation magazines or available in Public Libraries. One of the most informative sources of *Real* enthusiast talks is to be found — usually free of charge or for a very modest fee — in most public conveniences, although the source is more customarily associated with drying of the hands.

Taking Off

This is when the aircraft hares down the runway with the pilot's knuckles turning white as he frantically pulls back on the control column and the co-pilot, if there is one, calling out how many yards of runway are left, while the rest of the crew try to look unconcerned but sit very close to the nearest escape hatch. At some point before the end of the concrete speed will have enabled the wings to generate enough lift for the aircraft to take to the air. In machines like the Galaxy and fully loaded tankers, the curvature of the earth helps.

Tankers

The only aeroplanes that take-off with much more fuel than they will ever require. They then lay in wait to refuel other aircraft that took off without enough fuel to get where they wanted to go, or have decided to stay airborne for longer than they originally thought. Tanker crews are among the bravest (although others will argue that they are the silliest) flyers in the world. Tanker crews are usually in very strong positions to become prima donnas and it is best not to fall out with them, especially if you are in the receiving aircraft. The following is a true story:

In the early 1960s a Flight of F-105s equipped with rather primitive doppler navigational radar was over mid-Atlantic. The leader of the Flight was a know-it-all ace jet jockey. The tankers each had the services of a crack navigator and when

'Honest skip... there WERE three F4s when we went into that cloud.'

they arrived at the rendezvous there was no sign of the fighters, so they orbited well within 'the box'. Meanwhile, some way away the fighter leader calls the tankers and claims to be in the designated refuelling area. The tanker leader calls back.

Blindman Blue Flight, this is tanker Able 5. According to our plot you're north of us!'

There then follows a running verbal fight.

Fighter leader: 'You clowns are outta position. My doppler says so!'

Tanker leader: 'An I say you gotta head 180 degrees for 50 nm to reach us.'

Finally, tanker number 6 picks up the mike and broadcasts on the emergency channel:

'Attention, all fighters in the mid-Atlantic area, attention all fighters in the mid-Atlantic area... THIS IS GOD... THIS IS GOD... the tankers are right... the tankers are right... GOD out.'

Fighter leader: 'Ah... ummmm... tanker Able 5, say again vector *and* distance to your position.'

Undercarriage

In most cases the wheels under the aircraft that are supposed to be lowered before landing. It is now very rare for pilots to forget to do this, although they have to be reminded by flashing lights, horns, shouts from other crew members or in the case of single-seat aircraft, red flares fired from the ground. If they do forget the landing can be very spectacular, although it does of course save a lot of tyre wear. On one occasion during the Second World War a pilot was transferred to flying boats from heavy bombers. One day he decided to take his flying boat and visit his former colleagues. As he lined up to land at the airfield the runway controller, seeing a huge flying boat about to cut a furrow down his runway, fired off a red Very light. This reminded the pilot he was not flying an aircraft with wheels... he returned to his base, lined up and carried out a perfect cross-wind landing on his hull and floats... then, all smiles, stepped out of the flying boat straight into the sea.

Hang gliders and some micro-lights are the only aircraft to use the pilot's legs as an undercarriage... *not to be recommended.*

'What's the number of AA Relay get you home service?'

'I can't hear you sir... due to the noise from that horn.'

U-2 (Lockheed)

Without doubt the most famous aeroplane in history. Based on a British-designed torch (flashlight) battery, when it really mattered the *Power* (sic) failed and it came down in Russia much to everyone's surprise as it was supposed to be gathering samples from the atmosphere over the South Pacific. This was one of the biggest navigational errors in the history of aviation, and led to much acclaim from the Russians who were so impressed they eventually agreed to let the pilot name one of their own design fighters — The Yakovlev Yak 25F — Flashlight after the battery that failed. (This story was kindly supplied by the CIA).

USAF

After the Confederate Air Force (see under C); the biggest

By dispersing tankers in car parks, the USAF fool Russian spy satellites into thinking that western cars are getting BIGGER and BIGGER, and not everyone drives around in a VW.

They all came out of a little disc, led by a little green man chanting 'We're with the W******h.'

air force in the world. Believers in Flying Saucers claim 'UFOs are real, the USAF is an hallucination'. Aircraft which are believed to belong to this air force are now painted in such a low-visibility camouflage scheme that is indeed very hard to find out whether or not they do exist. At the time of writing neither CND nor the British Government were prepared to make any comment. The American Department of Defense, under the Freedom of Information Act (1980) simply confirmed that George *did* cut down his father's cherry tree.

Uplift

Please refer to Kayser Bonder, Berlie, or a dictionary of aerodynamics.

Vintage Aeroplanes

Some pedantic people will argue that flying and aviation have not existed long enough to have any established traditions... there are just habits. It is perhaps wise to adopt the terminology used in the 'old' car world so that we can at least include some definitions that have become regular parts of the aviation vocabulary, although it is very much a case of each to his own. Vintage is generally accepted to mean those built between the years 1917 and 1930. So corroded hulks of aluminium and fabric, usually with two sets of wings and enormous radial engines, that have been found on rubbish tips, in scrap yards or dug-up from reclaimed fenland, and are waiting to be rebuilt by enthusiast groups, are Vintage aeroplanes. But as with most things, the term has become abused and is often used to describe any aeroplane about which one or more people feel inclined to write to an enthusiast publication expressing horror that it (the subject matter) is about to be scrapped. This means that Vulcans, Victors, Seamews, Fireflies and VC 10s (if not required for conversion to tankers) can all

'I don't care if you never speak to me again.'

become Vintage aeroplanes, proving the pen is mightier than the scrap hammer.

Veteran Aeroplanes

These are rotting wooden hulks usually with two sets of wings and enormous radial engines, built between 1905 and 1917, that are waiting to be rebuilt by enthusiast groups. As the RAF was not formed until 1918 there can be *no* Veteran RAF machines, and as the poor old USAF did not come into being until 1948, they cannot have any Veteran or Vintage relics.

To overcome these shortcomings it is not uncommon to hear the term *Classic Aeroplanes* (in hushed whispers) used to describe both the V & V and those that don't fit either category. Therefore a 'Classic Aeroplane' can be a collection of rotting wood, corroded, aluminium, tatty fabric, bent sheet aluminium *et al,* that is awaiting rebuilding by an enthusiast group. Sometimes you will hear in even more hushed terms, a 'Classic Veteran Aircraft'. This is one from any period from 1903 to 1980 that has been recovered from any of the places previously mentioned, or even a great hole in the ground, and rebuilt so that it actually flies again. Most of these will be found in the hands of eccentric millionaires, or The Shuttleworth Collection which in essence amounts to the same thing.

—'V' Force

This was the British Government's answer to the present day American 'A Team' as seen on frequent ITV repeats. It was a group of bombers flown by intrepid birdmen, ready to fly at the slightest whim of the Prime Minister, to any troubled spot in the world and wash the British dirty linen in public. Hence it became known as the 'British Detergent'. This role was eventually handed over to the Royal Navy, as they were more at home in hot water, and in any case parts of the 'V' Bombers began to corrode. . . due no doubt to the use of the wrong washing powder, or the introduction of fabric softeners, and many preservation groups had their eyes on them thus giving the Chancellor the opportunity to make a quick pound or two for the Government's coffers.

Pilot to nav: 'Are you SURE this is Port Stanley?'

von Richthofen

Even if you have no interest in aviation of the First World War period, it is mandatory to have at least a nodding acquaintance with the legend of Manfred von Richthofen. Most collectors and museums, and every member of Cross & Cockade (especially the American Branch, or Chapter as they prefer it) has a piece of fabric from the Fokker Triplane he flew. This means the aircraft was a triplane of similar proportions to today's C-5 Galaxy. Failing this, they all have a part of the Camel (aircraft) that was supposed to have shot him down, or if you belong to the school of thought that it was an Australian infantryman who performed the evil deed, a clod of preserved mud taken from his boots.

Recent papers discovered in a loft in Brisbane prove that he was not, in fact, shot down, but landed quite voluntarily when he caught a smell of a tube of Fosters and after tasting it, couldn't go back to Carlsberg Lager, so was smuggled to Australia in a Billy-Can, where he carved a new career for himself by singing songs about kangaroos, and painting on large sheets of paper with a distemper brush. He also grew a beard to disguise his Teutonic features. Cross & Cockade will naturally deny this story, as to support it would affect sales of their von Richthofen memorabilia.

Variable Geometry

Since the days of Icarus, scientists have been trying to prove to pilots that wings are not really necessary for safe flight. In the days of the biplane they worked hard to get the second set of wings dropped, then later on the F-104 was introduced. But as long as some wing could be seen, pilots were happy.

The idea of a wing that could be seen on take off then gradually slid out of sight into the fuselage, was the next ploy, and in some cases seems to be working, although there are notable examples of a splinter group trying to preserve as much wing area as possible (Concorde, Vulcan and the

A-300 with everything hanging out). The fact that those Americans who have landed on the Moon did not need any wings seems to have cut very little ice with pilots and/or passengers, so VG is still in its infancy, and it is probably a long way off before wings can be (variably) swept under the fuselage for good. One advantage is that air show organizers can get more aeroplanes of this type into their static displays, but this is counter-productive as few people want to see rows and rows of F-111s, F-14s and Tornados, but a big advantage for the 'pros' is that it is something else for the pilot to remember. Just as most of them have become used to remembering to put wheels down, they now have to think about putting the wings out before landing. There is a reminder in the form of a horn, and this together with the undercarriage horn makes most cockpits sound something like a concert hall during the landing pattern. Pilots who have switched off both horns, then forgotten to extend their wings, have landed safely without wings which proves the scientists are right. Wings are *not* required for trouble-free flight...

Visibility

When there are no clouds and it is possible to see for miles, all pilots can fly; when the clouds are low and it is possible to see only a few yards, only Sergeant and ex-Sergeant pilots can fly. In the Service when it is a clear cloudless day, it is usually known as 'Flight Commanders' weather'.

NB, This is a Service type story, so a good initiative test for those aspiring to become *Real* enthusiasts is to get a full explanation from a Service pilot. But *don't* ask a Flight Commander!

Westland

A famous British (in fact the only one) company that makes helicopters, mostly to other people's designs. They are soon to produce 2,000 American Blackhawk helicopters. To whom they will sell these must remain one of the most closely guarded secrets of aviation, since the original American producers of the machine have only managed to sell 206 in three years, and these were to people who didn't really want them, but were — it is rumoured — ordered by a life-size latex puppet from a British TV show.

Westland never show a loss, they prefer the term 'negative profit', how their Chairman keeps his job with a 'negative profit' of some £93m is a secret that he could probably sell to a lot of British football club managers, and make himself more than Jeffrey Archer and Fredrick Forsyth combined.

Wind

The annual debate in the House of Commons on aviation and defence.

Wind Tunnel

This is a device through which wind is blown at various speeds to investigate aerodynamic theory. Some noticeable wind tunnels can be found at: most political party conferences, the opposition defence benches, Air Show organization committees meetings, Annual General Meetings of most aviation groups, places (mostly pubs) where air correspondents meet, on 'Top of the Pops', 'Dallas', 'News at Ten', 'This Week', 'Dynasty', 'The Archers', 'East Enders', 'Match of the Day', TV motor racing and Air Show documentaries, at The House of Commons, The House of Lords, The House of Pan and the House where the Brighouse & Rastrick Brass Band practice.

Wheels

In the pioneering days of aviation it was challenging to see how many sets of wings could be fitted to aeroplanes, today it is how many sets of wheels can be included in an aircraft's undercarriage. It was fashionable to have just two huge mainwheels and a tail wheel, then it was two slimline main wheels with tyres inflated to 500 psi, then the tyre manufacturers began to put their thinking caps on. Looking through an old wartime picture book (not many of them can read) one expert found a picture of a Me 323 with what seemed to be hundreds of tiny wheels. 'Eureka!' he cried,

'How should I know what ALL the tyre pressures are.'

and from then on plans were afoot, and there has been no
going back. So today aeroplanes like the '747, C-5,
Starlifter, Tristar and so on, have enough wheels to make
every tyre manufacturer a millionaire every time they make a
heavy landing. Strategic distribution of FOD ensures that
punctures are a regular part of the scene. The rubber
companies employed well-known publicity agents to spread
damaging stories about water and aeroplanes not mixing,
which is why flying boats gradually faded from the aviation
scene. The USAF and the Red Arrows are the tyre
companies' best customers.

Women Pilots

The delicate touch, high intelligence level, superb physical
shape and understanding of all things mechanical, makes
women the best pilots in the world. Men have always denied
them the right to enter this field, which is a gross injustice
that should be put right (the author and cartoonist have to
keep SOME friends!).

X-Planes

It was customary in 1945 to name all experimental aircraft X-planes, particularly in the USA where there were aircraft like the X-5, X-15 and so on. In England they tended to think that aviation had reached the limit of human endurance and the Government of the day banned all experimental manned aircraft that were planned to investigate supersonic flight (*this is true*). So X-planes took on a new meaning in the UK where the term referred to a pile of scrap or a hole in the ground. This is probably when the very first seeds of the preservation movement were sown. It also led to a new approach by those who just will *not* accept that the biplane is dead; the result is that in the film *Star Wars* the 'X-wing' fighter made its debut.

If you study this carefully you will see that it is in fact a biplane with its four sets of wings arranged in a different configuration. Watch out for the Jedi otherwise before long a secret group will be started to prove that the Tiger Moth with an RB211 engine would be a suitable MRCA for replacing the Tornado. *You have been warned.*

X-Servicemen/women

The very salt of the earth providing you keep them off the odd tipple. Those of you who can remember as far back as Enthusiast Groups will recall Air Gunners' and Aircrew Associations; these are all of course ex-Servicemen but the parties now under discussion are, in the main, not within that category. They can be identified because they knew Max Bygraves when he was a boy. All ex-Service personnel have a host of stories about flying and the RAF, even if the nearest they ever came to an aeroplane was the donation of elastic from a pair of unmentionables to power a balsa and tissue creation of a small brother, nephew, cousin, etc.

These all improve with telling but usually include: a bad take-off, a bad landing, getting lost, the pilot being sick, dying or having a heart-attack during the flight, an attack by

a Staffel or even Geschwader of Ju 88s over the Bay of
Biscay, or more often than not, a WAAF riding on the tail
of a Spitfire.

Have fun listening to them, buy another tipple, and switch
to NAAFI tea and the antics of Ginger Saltash and Mary
Raleigh from Nottingham, behind Hangar 4 during Fire
Picket duty. Likely to be much more believable and certainly
nearer the truth as well as very exciting as the evening wears
on, and Mary begins to wish she hadn't donated *that* piece
of elastic.

X-Films

Among the films made about aviation that fit the true
meaning of this category, (refer to definitions of the British
Board of Film Censors if you are in any doubt) are:

Mosquito Squadron,	*First of the Few,*
Target for Tonight,	*Strategic Air Command,*
Angels One Five,	*The War Lover,*
Hell's Angels,	*The Blue Max,*
Flying Leathernecks,	*The Malta Story,*
The Sound Barrier	*and Mary Poppins.*

Youth Movements

As with nearly all things, there is always a twist in the tail. By now you have nearly become a *Real* enthusiast, but be very wary, you are not quite there. Be very, very careful about the biggest danger to all aspiring aviation buffs: Members of the Air Training Corps, or ATC for short. These pimply faced masters, and now misses, cannot be taken on face value, they will quote you wing-loading factors, static thrust, every aspect of aerodynamics, the ins-and-outs of RADAR, heat-seeking missiles, the histories of every aircraft built, and some not built, in fact *everything* to do with aviation. They will almost certainly also be crack marksmen, and faster over 220 yards than you are over 25 yards. Forget their angelic looks, and avoid any reference to your interest in aviation within their earshot. It is much better to claim a deep and avid interest in the letters of the younger Pliny; even then you might occasionally be on dangerous ground.

Air Scouts can be equally dangerous and will also know a lot about knots and starting fires by rubbing two aviation enthusiasts together.

Yawing

This is an unstable movement about the normal axis, and should be adopted if one of the above is encountered; it is a good way of escaping without too many awkward questions being asked.

'WHAT time are those Zulus coming?'

Zulu Time

This is a term that has been borrowed from the Army. At Rorke's Drift the South Wales Borderers (or whoever they were) expected the attacking Zulus to arrive at dawn. They were an hour late, and if Second Lieutenant Michael Caine had not been alert, all the garrison would have been slaughtered (not many people knew that). When the powers that be were looking for another element to confuse everyone in the world of aviation, they chose — as a mark of respect for the Army's achievement — to use the term Zulu time. This has succeeded beyond their wildest imagination because very few people now really know whether they are ahead or behind GMT — except, of course, the Zulus, and as there are very few Zulu pilots it doesn't really matter.

Zero (Mitsubishi)

There was very little to this Japanese fighter (hence its name), apart from a bamboo cane framework covered with rice-paper. Nonetheless, it was very successful and one example that completed fifty Kamikaze missions in the hands of the same pilot, Chicken Chow-Mein, is preserved in Tokyo by the Japanese equivalent of the British Aircraft Preservation Group.

Zero-Zero Ejection Seat

A special type of deck-chair which enables a quick getaway to be made when the attendant is seen approaching for money, and also useful at Bank Holidays when some of the more outrageous youth of the country decide to spend a day at the seaside. Can be very helpful at Air Shows, so every attempt should be made to get one, but please note, they are *not* allowed on the top decks of open top buses now frequently used for photographic purposes.

We were trying to get that car moved, and when we came back, the rest had gone.

ZZZZZzzzzzzzzzzzzzzzzz . . .

Symbol used by navigators to show they were asleep during
the briefing... If you have got this far, you should now
have a basic grounding on which to build your career as a
Real aviation enthusiast. If you require more... hey you...
are you awake?... oh well, I guess there is always gardening
or shopping to occupy summer Saturdays and Sundays...
No, don't wake up, I'll see myself out... Have a nice day!